P9-DBT-910

AGENT MOST WANTED

AGENT MOST WANTED

the NEVER-BEFORE-TOLD STORY of the MOST DANGEROUS SPY of WORLD WAR II

SONIA PURNELL

FOR SUE, 1951–2017.
COURAGE COMES IN MANY FORMS.

VIKING
An imprint of Penguin Random House LLC, New York

First published in the United States of America by Viking,
an imprint of Penguin Random House LLC, 2022

Photo credits
Page viii: Lorna Catling Collection; Page 4: Lorna Catling Collection; Page 7: Lorna Catling Collection; Page 8: Lorna Catling Collection; Page 12: Lorna Catling Collection; Page 15: Lorna Catling Collection; Page 21: Lorna Catling Collection; Page 30: Lorna Catling Collection; Page 52: David Harrison Collection; Page 58: Via *No Cloak, No Dagger* by Ben Cowburn, Jarrolds, 1960; Page 67: The National Archives, UK; Page 79: David Harrison Collection; Page 83: Lorna Catling Collection; Page 90: National Archives and Records Administration; Page 101: Via *No Banners* by Jack Thomas, WH Allen, 1955; Page 106: The National Archives, UK; Page 107: The National Archives, UK; Page 123: Lorna Catling Collection; Page 128: Via *Le Chambon-sur-Lignon sous l'occupation* by Pierre Fayol, L'Harmattan, 1990; Page 135: The National Archives, UK; Page 144: Copyright collection privée. Courtesy of Lieu de Mémoire au Chambon-sur-Lignon; Page 146: Copyright Jeffrey Bass; Page 148: Copyright collection privée. Courtesy of Lieu de Mémoire au Chambon-sur-Lignon; Page 154: Courtesy of Lieu de Mémoire au Chambon-sur-Lignon; Page 159: Courtesy of Lieu de Mémoire au Chambon-sur-Lignon; Page 162: Via *Le Chambon-sur-Lignon sous l'occupation* by Pierre Fayol, L'Harmattan, 1990; Page 171: Lorna Catling Collection; Page 178 top: Courtesy of Lorna Catling and John Hall; Page 178 bottom: Courtesy of Lorna Catling and John Hall; Page 184: Lorna Catling Collection; Page 187: Copyright collection privée. Courtesy of Lieu de Mémoire au Chambon-sur-Lignon

Visit us online at penguinrandomhouse.com.

Library of Congress Cataloging-in-Publication Data is available.

Book manufactured in Canada

ISBN 9780593350546

1 3 5 7 9 10 8 6 4 2

FRI

Design by Kate Renner
Text set in ITC Cheltenham Pro

It is from numberless diverse acts of courage and belief that human history is shaped. Each time a man stands up for an ideal, or acts to improve the lot of others, or strikes out against injustice, he sends forth a tiny ripple of hope, and crossing each other from a million different centers of energy and daring, those ripples build a current that can sweep down the mightiest walls.

ROBERT F. KENNEDY

CONTENTS

Virginia as a young woman.

PROLOGUE

May 1940. France was falling to Germany. Ten million women, children, and old men—the largest exodus of refugees in history—were fleeing the armies of Adolf Hitler's Nazi regime. Roads were littered with burned-out cars, possessions, and bodies. But the horde kept coming: a never-ending line too hungry, tired, and fearful to stop.

A French army ambulance wove through the crowd, its driver a thirty-four-year-old American volunteer. Private Virginia Hall often ran low on fuel and medicine, but she just kept going. Even when enemy German aircraft screamed overhead, dive-bombing the convoys all around her, torching the cars and cratering the roads. Even when the planes machine-gunned the ditches where women and children were taking shelter. Even when her left hip complained from her constantly pressing on the clutch with her prosthetic foot.

In the midst of destruction, she had never felt so thrillingly alive.

Virginia's service as an ambulance driver was an apprenticeship for her future mission against the occupying German forces. In an age when women barely figured in warfare, she went on to create a daredevil role for herself involving espionage, sabotage, and resistance behind enemy lines.

As an undercover agent, Virginia operated in the shadows, and that was where she was happy. Her closest allies knew neither her real name nor her nationality. She seemed to have no home or family or regiment, just a burning desire to defeat the Nazis. Constantly changing her appearance and mannerisms, surfacing without notice then disappearing again, she remained a mystery throughout the war and in some ways after it too.

When the battle for France's liberation from Hitler's tyranny began, in 1944, the underground Resistance fighters she had equipped, trained, and sometimes commanded exceeded all expectations and helped bring about complete and final victory for the Allies: Britain, the United States, and the Soviet Union. But even that was not enough for Virginia Hall.

CHAPTER 1

DINDY

Mrs. Barbara Hall had raised Virginia, her only daughter and youngest child, born on April 6, 1906, in the expectation that she would marry well. It was Virginia's duty to restore the family to the heights of Baltimore society by marrying into money. But Virginia did not oblige. Tall and rangy, with sparkly nut-brown eyes and a melting smile (when she chose to use it), she was a free-spirited girl with a strong independent streak. "I must have liberty," she proclaimed in her school yearbook in 1924, at the age of eighteen.

She took pleasure in defying convention. At a time when girls traditionally wore only skirts, she chose trousers and shirts whenever she could, and enjoyed hunting with a rifle, skinning rabbits, and riding horses bareback. Once she wore a bracelet of live snakes into school. It was clear that the fearless young "Dindy," as her family called her, had no intention of settling down.

Dindy's classmates recognized her gifts for organization and initiative. They viewed her as their natural leader and elected her

Virginia (right) as a little girl, with her father, Ned, and brother, John.

class president, editor in chief, captain of sports, and even "class prophet." Her father, Edwin Lee Hall (known as Ned), a well-to-do Baltimore banker and movie theater owner, allowed his daughter the freedom to be herself. But her mother, Barbara, had quite different views, and determined that her daughter would forsake adventure for the prize of a rich husband and a fashionable household. So, at the age of nineteen, Virginia dutifully became engaged to be married. Like many young society women, she seemed destined for a confined and domestic life.

However, rebellion was in the air. Confident young women,

the independence-loving, modern "flappers," scandalized their elders by cutting their hair short into bobs and dancing to jazz music. Some rejected the restrictions of traditional marriage, preferring to make their own way in society—especially after 1920, when American women won the right to vote. The prospect of a quiet life at home was stifling to Virginia when the outside world offered such enticing new freedoms. And so—to her fiancé's indignation—she ditched him and went to university. (She made the right decision; he went on to have three unhappy marriages.)

Yet the studious atmosphere of Radcliffe College, which she attended for a year in 1924, bored Virginia, and in 1925 she transferred to Barnard College in Manhattan. She enjoyed the bright lights of New York City, particularly the theaters on Broadway, but her college tutors rated her only "an average student." Virginia knew she needed a college education to get a job as a diplomat—representing her country abroad was her dream career—so she persuaded her parents that she would do better if she could study abroad.

Like many well-to-do East Coast Americans at the time, Virginia set her sights on Paris as her gateway to independence. In 1926, at twenty years of age, she enrolled at the École Libre des Sciences Politiques. She discovered in Paris a thrilling scene of art, literature, and music, and mixed with actresses, race car drivers, intellectuals, and budding politicians in cafés and jazz clubs. Here, at last, she felt she could be herself.

Her free-spirited lifestyle continued when she moved, in the autumn of 1927, to Vienna to study languages, economics, and journalism. In contrast to her time as a student in New York, she thrived in her classes, and she also found plenty of time to soak up the city's vibrant atmosphere.

The elegantly dressed young American attracted plenty of male attention, especially from a dashing Polish army officer named Emil, who escorted her on romantic walks along the river Danube. Emil adored Virginia's free spirit and because of this won her heart in a way that no one had before.

However, Ned, seemingly egged on by Barbara, was against his daughter having a relationship with a foreigner from an uncertain background and certainly against the possibility of her settling in Europe. He told her to break up with Emil. Even though she was distraught, the normally willful Virginia obeyed her beloved father. She never saw Emil again, although she kept a photograph of him for many years.

Virginia's time as a student in Europe instilled in her a deep and abiding love of France, which she called her "second country." She also honed her portfolio of foreign languages: most usefully French and German, but also Spanish, Italian, and Russian. She became well versed in European culture, geography, and, crucially, politics. It was the late 1920s, and fascism was on the rise in Europe. In Germany, Italy, and Austria, she witnessed the growing power of violent and authoritarian groups seeking to control society.

Virginia returned home to Maryland in July 1929, and attended

George Washington University in Washington, D.C., where she studied French and economics. Her grades were good enough to apply to the State Department to become a diplomat. With her languages and extensive academic study abroad, she expected to succeed. The fact that at the time only six out of fifteen hundred Foreign Service officers were female should have been fair warning: Virginia's application was rejected. Refusing to accept defeat, however, she decided to enter by what she called the "back door."

Around that time, in January 1931, Ned suffered a massive heart attack, collapsing on the pavement outside his office. He died a few hours later. His loss at just fifty-nine was a cruel blow to his family, and perhaps to Virginia most of all. Ned had doted on his daring young Dindy, indulging her fondness for traditionally male pursuits such as hunting, and even buying his daughter her own gun.

Virginia was expected to settle down to a quiet life with her mother and her brother and his family, at the family home of Box Horn Farm, near Baltimore. Barbara no doubt hoped that Virginia would also now finally agree to marry, but after the independent lifestyle she had enjoyed in Europe, such

The Hall family home, Box Horn Farm, near Baltimore, Maryland.

A teenaged Virginia, surrounded by pigeons.

a claustrophobic arrangement was intolerable. Soon Virginia was applying for secretarial jobs in the diplomatic service—the "back door" she had previously mentioned.

After seven months at home, she landed a post at the US embassy in Warsaw, Poland. She had finally broken into the ranks of the State Department, but despite all her studies and all her ambition, it was in a lowly position. Nevertheless, Virginia made an instant impression, conducting her duties with flair and initiative, and soon taking on more responsibility. She coded and decoded confidential telegrams, dealt with the mail, processed diplomatic visas, and sent reports back to Washington on the increasingly tense political situation.

After a couple of years in Poland, in April 1933, she transferred to Smyrna, Turkey, but she found that her duties there were much the same as in Warsaw—and Turkey was of less strategic interest to the US than Poland, which shared a border with Nazi Germany. On the other hand, it was a perfect posting for someone with Virginia's love of the outdoor life. The lagoons and salt marshes of the Gediz River Delta were famous for pelicans and flamingos, and soon after her arrival she began organizing groups to go shooting for snipe—a popular species of bird.

On the clear and mild morning of Friday, December 8, Virginia set off for a day's hunting. She was to relive her actions that day for the rest of her life, and would never forgive her own carelessness. Perhaps it was her eagerness to be the first of her group to bag a bird that persuaded her not to engage the safety catch on her gun. Looking intently to the sky, she stumbled over a wire fence running through the reeds. As she fell, her gun slipped off her shoulder and got caught in her ankle-length coat. She reached out to grab it. In so doing, she fired a round at point-blank range into her left foot.

The wound was serious. The shotgun cartridge had been large, blunt, and full of round lead pellets, which were now deeply embedded in her flesh. Virginia lost consciousness as a slick of blood spread out in the muddy delta waters around her. Her friends tried to stanch the bleeding, then carried her to the car and dashed to the local hospital.

For the next three weeks, Virginia appeared to be recovering well, but a severe infection was seeping into her wound. Just before Christmas, she deteriorated rapidly, and the head of the American Hospital in Istanbul was urgently summoned, along with two nurses. By the time they arrived, after a twenty-four-hour train journey, Virginia's foot was swelling up and turning black. Her body was racked with waves of ferocious pain. It was gangrene. In the days before antibiotics, there was no effective medical treatment for infection. By Christmas Day, Virginia was on the brink of death. In a last-ditch bid to save her, the surgeons amputated her left leg below the knee.

The operation was a success, but her fight was far from over. One night, delirious with fever, Virginia had what she would later describe as a vision. The ghost of her father appeared at her bedside bearing a simple message. He told her that she must not give up and that "it was her duty to survive." She never forgot her father's words, and talked often over the years about how he had urged her to fight for her life. Miraculously, she pulled through, but pain would be her unceasing companion for the rest of her days.

CHAPTER 2

LIVING WITH CUTHBERT

On June 21, 1934, Virginia arrived home in the United States by ship. Her family met her at the pier and watched as she limped gingerly toward them. The Turkish doctors had given her only the most basic wooden leg, and she needed crutches to get around. She was admitted to the hospital for a series of what were called "repair operations," and was fitted with a new prosthetic leg. It was modern by 1930s standards, held in place by leather straps and corsetry around her waist. However, in hot weather the leather chafed her skin raw, and it blistered and bled. Despite being hollow, the painted wooden leg and its aluminum foot weighed in at a hefty eight pounds. Virginia gave it the pet name "Cuthbert," but she never said why.

Over the summer at Box Horn Farm, still battling persistent infections and the storm clouds of depression, Virginia taught herself to walk again, and regained her spirits relaxing on the veranda and helping to feed the sheep, horses, and goats. By November she was itching to return to work and secured a new posting at the

US consulate in Venice, Italy, where she set up home in a historic palazzo with a sweeping view over the Grand Canal.

Venice could not have been less suitable for an amputee, and when she first arrived, Virginia looked with horror upon its slippery cobbled passages and four hundred humpbacked bridges—many with steps—over its 177 canals. Not to be deterred, she quickly devised an ingenious solution: she bought herself a gondola. A local man, Angelo, who was devoted to her, showed her how to row it and was there to help her when the waters were rough. She was developing a knack for recruiting people who, charmed by her courage and lack of complaining, would go out of their way to help her.

Virginia rowing a gondola in Venice, Italy.

Once again, Virginia impressed her superiors at the US consulate. Anxious to prove her worth, she was soon handling the more complex and delicate tasks usually given to career diplomats rather than clerks like her. She even stood in for the vice consul when he was away. Staying busy, she had noticed, was one way to keep depression at bay.

The mid-1930s was a time of great poverty and increasing

political extremism across the world. Authoritarian dictators had seized power in several European countries. In Germany, Adolf Hitler was worshipped by millions, Benito Mussolini brutally governed Italy (Virginia's host country), General Francisco Franco was the strongman of Spain, and Joseph Stalin dominated the Soviet Union, as Russia was known at the time.

Virginia found herself in a ringside seat as the ideal of democracy became increasingly fragile. A rare exception was her home country, where President Franklin D. Roosevelt's New Deal offered a combination of relief programs and public works projects that provided desperately needed support and employment.

Horrified by the tide of totalitarianism rising all around her in Europe, Virginia yearned to be involved in diplomatic efforts to stop it. In late 1936, she decided to try again to get a job as a diplomat. With her five years' overseas service as a State Department clerk, she was no longer required to take the written exam: an interview would suffice. Confident that this would play to her strengths, she sailed back to the United States in January 1937 to pursue her application. She knew she had the support of her bosses in Venice and was feeling optimistic.

Now thirty and having served in US embassies and consulates in three different countries, she had much to offer in local political knowledge. However, her application was rejected. An obscure rule barring amputees from diplomacy—otherwise rarely enforced—was given as the reason. Virginia attempted to prove that her work had in no way been affected by her disability, but her efforts were in vain. She returned to Venice with her spirits crushed.

Her supporters attempted to have the decision overruled. One of them, Colonel E. M. House, even took it upon himself to lobby President Roosevelt, an old friend. He told Roosevelt that Virginia was a "gentlewoman of great intelligence" and a "credit to our country" who was the victim of an "injustice." Despite her injury, she lived an active life, including rowing, swimming, and horseback riding, and she had also "kept up her work," but had been told that she could never progress to the diplomatic corps.

On February 4, 1938, the president asked for a briefing about Virginia's rejection from Secretary of State Cordell Hull, who had personally ruled against Virginia. It seems that Hull was angered by the lobbying that had occurred on Virginia's behalf. He told Roosevelt that Virginia's disability hampered her performance, and that she was not up to the demands of a diplomatic position. Apparently ignoring the glowing reports from the consulate in Venice, Hull agreed she might make a "fine career girl," but only as a secretary. Roosevelt lived with his own disability—his legs were paralyzed by polio—and it had not prevented him from reaching the highest office in the country. Yet, ironically, he saw no reason to give Virginia a chance.

In what seems to have been a deliberate punishment for appealing the decision, Virginia was soon ordered to leave Venice and report for duty at the US legation, or diplomatic office, in Tallinn, the far-flung capital of Estonia. On top of that, when

Virginia's passport photograph and signature.

Virginia requested to be routed through Paris—only slightly out of the way—so she could get urgent repairs to her prosthetic leg, she was told that her expenses would not be reimbursed. Living up to her rebellious reputation, Virginia decided to travel independently to the French capital, where she picked up again with old friends.

Few in Paris knew she had suffered an accident. They certainly had no idea that the thick stockings she wore, even in the spring sunshine, helped to disguise her prosthetic leg and cushion her stump to minimize pain and bleeding. Virginia had been brought up never to discuss money, feelings, or health, and to always hold back a little from the crowd. Keeping silent about her problems—and her secrets—came naturally.

Virginia arrived in Tallinn at the end of June, and started work at the same two-thousand-dollar-a-year salary she'd received since being hired seven years before. She had never had a pay raise in all of that time. She found a different kind of reward in the hunting that was available in the vast, virgin forests of Estonia, and she wasted no time getting licenses to shoot birds, including capercaillie, grouse, and pheasant. She was determined that her accident would not deprive her of the sport of hunting.

The low-grade work, however, bored her. Europe was spinning toward war, and she was stuck answering the phone and filing papers. Fearful of the world's future, all hopes of promotion dashed, pigeonholed as a disabled woman of no importance, in March 1939, Virginia resigned from the State Department. For all her ambition, her career had proved little more rewarding than the old-fashioned marriage she had rejected. How could she break through the constrictions of her life to do something really worthwhile? How could she prove that her survival against the odds had been for a purpose?

Virginia stayed in Estonia for some months after her resignation, but when Germany attacked its neighbor Poland on September 1, 1939, she left for London before it was too late to get out of the country. Britain and France had declared war on September 3, 1939, and her plan was to volunteer for the women's branch of the British Army, the Auxiliary Territorial Service. But when she turned up at the recruitment office, the sergeant told her that foreigners were not welcome. It was yet another rejection. Most people would have given up at this point and returned to the safety of the United States. But Virginia Hall was not most people. She sailed for Paris.

In February 1940, her persistence paid off when she was able to sign up with the French Ninth Artillery Regiment as an ambulance driver. The Ninth was one of the few military corps open to women volunteers—and to foreigners. Finally, Virginia had a chance to play her part. On May 6, she reported for duty.

Four days later, German tanks surged over the border into France, taking the ill-prepared French troops by surprise. It took only a couple of weeks for the French, Belgian, and British armies in the area to be cut off by the advancing German army. To Virginia's dismay, most of her ambulance unit panicked, abandoning the wounded where they lay and leaving her to work largely alone. But then, she realized, many of their officers and civilian leaders had also fled their responsibilities. Even the French government deserted the capital, Paris, on June 10, escaping south to Bordeaux, where it collapsed in disarray.

When the Germans poured, unchallenged, into Paris at dawn, four days later, Virginia was already on her way to the Loire Valley, deep in the heart of France. She had heard that a determined French colonel was still collecting the wounded and driving them the two hundred miles to hospitals in Paris. He was in urgent need of help, and Virginia responded to the call.

For several weeks she relayed soldiers to the capital, where she had to apply for fuel coupons and passes from the German authorities, newly installed under giant swastika flags at the Hôtel Meurice. As a supposedly neutral American, she was permitted greater freedoms than the French she worked alongside, a fact she did not fail to notice. An idea began to form in her head.

On June 22, 1940, France's new leader, Philippe Pétain, signed a truce with Hitler, signaling his country's complete defeat. The north and west of the country, including Paris, were occupied by the Germans and became known as the "Occupied Zone." The south—the "Free Zone"—remained unoccupied by German troops, for the time being, but was officially governed by the Germans' puppet, Pétain, from headquarters in the spa town of Vichy, in the southeast of the country. Although French, Pétain effectively took orders from Hitler, even if he pretended otherwise.

With most of Europe occupied by or allied with Germany, Britain was now standing alone against Hitler. But how long could it survive? America, still recovering from the losses of World War I and the Great Depression, refused to be drawn into the war, but Virginia, having seen the realities of fascism and Nazi aggression with her own eyes, planned to continue the fight. She was convinced that it would not be long before the French rose up again and reclaimed their freedom and their country. She vowed to help them—and to do that, she first had to get to Britain.

CHAPTER 3

A CHANCE MEETING

British secret agent George Bellows was in a dusty Spanish border town on a white-hot day toward the end of August 1940. Spain was officially neutral in the war, and each day thousands of refugees from France streamed over the border, any one of whom might have vital information about what was happening under the Nazi regime. The British government had been virtually in the dark about the fate of its closest continental neighbor since its troops had been evacuated from Dunkirk, in northern France, earlier that summer. Nearly all its spies in France either had been killed, could no longer operate, or had fled.

Bellows's eye was caught by a striking red-haired woman with an American accent who was making inquiries at the ticket office. Intrigued, he struck up a conversation with her. She had come from France and wished to take a train to Portugal and then travel to Britain by ship. Bellows introduced himself as a salesman experienced in the challenges of wartime travel and offered to help.

Virginia told Bellows about her time driving an ambulance

across France, often alone and frequently under fire. She recounted, in matter-of-fact detail, how conditions were rapidly deteriorating across France, and angrily described curfews and food shortages in the Occupied Zone, widespread arrests, and an incident at a car factory where workers had been lined up against the wall and shot.

As he listened to her impassioned account, Bellows was astonished by Virginia's courage, her powers of observation, and, most of all, her desire to help the French. Trusting his instincts, he gave her the phone number of a "friend in London" who could help find her a worthwhile role, and urged her to call him. The State Department might not have appreciated her qualities, but Bellows knew he had just encountered someone exceptional.

He did not give anything away, and Virginia seems to have assumed she would be driving ambulances again once she reached England. But the phone number belonged to Nicolas Bodington, a senior officer in the French (F) Section of a brand-new British intelligence service, the Special Operations Executive (SOE). This agency was established after troops evacuated from Dunkirk. It relied on an "ungentlemanly" style of warfare, based in large part on the paramilitary tactics of Irish Republican fighters during the Anglo-Irish war of 1919 to 1921. That war showed that it was possible for a few resolute gunmen—a resistance movement—to defeat regular military troops. SOE agents were expected to do as Irish paramilitary leaders had done: to inspire, assist, and direct the local population to rise up against their oppressors when the time was right, and to eliminate without mercy those who got in the way.

Virginia, circa 1926.

Agents from the existing British spy service had been trained to gather intelligence but to avoid taking direct action. SOE agents would be different. They would observe, yes, but they would also recruit, train, and lead paramilitary guerrilla fighters. As one writer put it: if agents from the famed British intelligence service MI6 (Military Intelligence, Section 6) spotted enemy troops crossing a bridge, they would observe them from a distance and estimate their number. SOE would blow up the bridge.

However, SOE was struggling to find volunteers brave enough for the job. Traditionally, British military intelligence recruited upper-class young men raised on adventure stories about the British Empire, but this preference for social class over ability meant that their agents were no match for the barbarism of Hitler's regime, the Third Reich.

When Virginia arrived in London, she seems to have had a change of heart and to have been reluctant to put her mother through any more worry. Perhaps she doubted that she could really make herself useful. Instead of using the phone number Bellows had given her, she presented herself at the US embassy in London as a former State Department employee and asked for a temporary job while she waited to be able to travel home.

The embassy did not make her welcome; after all, she had resigned from the State Department once before. True, her up-to-date knowledge of France was invaluable, and she wrote a detailed report on matters such as the curfew and food shortages, but the State Department was most interested in her linguistic and typing skills. The embassy's military expert needed a secretary, and within a couple of weeks, Virginia was behind a typewriter again.

Weeks passed. She was still hoping for more worthwhile work, but finally, shortly before Christmas, a resigned Virginia decided to book her passage home. However, more than a year had passed since her resignation from the State Department in Estonia, and so she was no longer eligible for an official ticket. Because of the war, no others were available. She was stuck in London, during what is known as the Blitz, a series of nightly bombings by German aircraft that terrorized the city.

With few other options, Virginia dug out the telephone number Bellows had given her months previously. The call was answered by Nicolas Bodington, who invited her to dinner. On a bitterly cold night in January 1941, Virginia met Bodington and his American wife, Elizabeth, at their stylish home in the upscale area of Mayfair.

Behind tightly shut blackout curtains, the Bodingtons treated Virginia to as fine a meal and as warm a fire as wartime conditions allowed. The Blitz meant that Londoners had to cover all their windows and doors with heavy fabric to block any light from escaping that might help the enemy locate their targets.

Virginia had no idea that Nicolas Bodington was a senior officer in SOE. Nor did she know that he was exasperated by his section's failure to infiltrate a single agent into France after six months of trying. But she enchanted him with talk about her own plans to return to France now that she could not get home to America.

The next morning, Bodington rushed to work at the top-secret SOE offices on Baker Street. In a state of considerable excitement, he took the wobbly elevator up to the fifth floor, and dictated an urgent memo to his superior: "It strikes me that this lady, a native of Baltimore, might well be used for a mission."

Because Virginia was American, she was not officially involved in the war. There would be no need to sneak her into France with a challenging clandestine sea landing or parachute drop. Nor would her strongly accented French be a problem. She could pose as an American journalist, which would also explain her need to travel around and ask questions.

At the time, however, the British government had forbidden women from frontline military service, having been advised that women were particularly vulnerable if taken prisoner, because they were not protected by international laws on warfare. Within SOE itself, there was "considerable hostility" at every level to the idea of women in the field. They could only work in support—as decoders, typists, or couriers. Furthermore, Virginia was American;

her country was not at war with Germany. Could she be trusted? It was standard intelligence policy to recruit only British citizens or people from countries already invaded by the Nazis.

It looked as though Virginia's disability had now become almost the only thing *not* to count against her. There is no mention of her prosthetic leg in Virginia's file, and SOE seems not to have been bothered by it. Because of her time in the ambulance service, her superiors knew she was able to drive, and when asked if she could ride a horse, sail a boat, shoot, scale mountains, ski, or cycle, she answered yes, yes, yes, yes, yes, and yes. On the other hand, it was true that she could not run, a most important skill for a secret agent.

In the end, Bodington won the day, arguing that a recruit's nationality was unimportant, so long as they were loyal to the British war effort. And with the urgent need to get agents into France, the fact that one of the very few plausible candidates was a woman would simply have to be overlooked. SOE's emergency was Virginia's breakthrough.

How could Virginia, a lover of adventure stuck in a dead-end job in what she considered a dead-end life, resist such an offer? And so, on April 1, 1941, Agent 3844 started to prepare for her secret mission as a liaison officer (class A). Virginia was the first female agent in F Section and the first liaison officer of any sex.

Her appointment demonstrated that F Section had faith in a woman who had for so long been belittled or ignored. But her superiors also knew that it was all a huge gamble. No one knew if the desk clerk from Baltimore really had what it took to survive even a few days in the field. SOE simply didn't know whether she would find support in France for Britain to continue the fight against Germany, or plain hostility. If there was support, could the French people be organized into effective paramilitary networks to resist fascism? Or were they now cowed servants of the Nazi regime? SOE had no idea whether an agent could stay alive there long enough to report back.

Virginia's mission was confirmed as "Liaison and Intelligence in Vichy France." Others in SOE, although not technically soldiers, were granted an equivalent military rank to underline their authority to give orders. Virginia was not, perhaps because her disability meant she would fail the necessary medical test. It was an omission that would dog her for the rest of her mission, because it made her authority easier to question. For now, plain Miss Hall's orders were to report on the situation on the ground and to help other agents who would follow her to France.

Over a few days, in a heavily guarded house in southern England, Virginia learned the basics of coding and guerrilla warfare: How to spread pro-British propaganda. How to use cover names and code names in the field. The "importance of looking natural and ordinary" while doing "unnatural and extraordinary things." She learned how to use reflections in windows to check if someone was following her, and if someone was, how to lose them by doubling back on her path. She learned when to move to a new home, how to make invisible inks (urine comes up well when subjected to heat), and how to avoid attracting attention with mannerisms like a distinctive laugh. She learned how to hide tiny containers of microfilm in her navel or rectum—or, as she discovered, a handy slot in the heel of her prosthetic foot.

She learned how to leave no trace when going through files or desk drawers, even how to replace the dust on a smooth surface. And how to approach a guarded house without making a noise. A retired burglar taught her to pick a lock. Already familiar with handling a gun, she now learned to fire a range of weapons. There was very little if any training for the primary mission—building a resistance network behind enemy lines in a foreign country—because no one had really done it before.

Due to the almost total lack of up-to-date intelligence from France, there was no way to prepare her fully for the dangers in the field. SOE officers in London didn't have the first clue how ruthless the Germans would be. "At the start . . . we all thought of the whole business as a game," recalled one early agent, who rapidly realized the truth. "A serious, deadly one, but a game nevertheless. There was amusement, excitement and adventure." Virginia would either learn fast on the job . . . or get herself killed.

CHAPTER 4

FACING THE ENEMY

In May 1941, while Virginia was awaiting clearance to enter the field, SOE finally succeeded in parachuting its first two agents into France. They were both men, and both French—fighting for their country's freedom by allying themselves with the British. Pierre de Vomécourt (code-named Lucas) was SOE's first organizer of a network, or circuit, of agents. Georges Bégué was its first radio operator and therefore its sole direct link with France.

At the time, there were no cell phones or satellites. Written letters could take weeks to arrive, and in wartime, they often did not arrive at all. SOE radio operators were known as "pianists" for their speed in tapping out messages in Morse code, beeps jokingly referred to as "music." The messages, which also used secret codes to prevent the Germans from deciphering what they said, were beamed over radio waves to receiving stations in England. There was a desperate need for information at this point in the war; just two men could hardly expect to begin to cover a country of 250,000 square miles. Virginia's presence was urgently required.

On August 23, 1941, she boarded a ship for Lisbon, and from there took a train to France, via Spain. No one in London gave her more than a fifty-fifty chance of surviving even her first few days in the field. For all her qualities, dispatching a one-legged thirty-five-year-old desk clerk on a blind mission into wartime France was an almost insane risk. If she was to be successful, she would have to lead her double life to perfection and avoid capture at all costs.

TWO YEARS TO the day since the start of the war, on September 3, 1941, a tall, confident woman with flame-red hair arrived in Vichy, the headquarters of Pétain's puppet government. She registered her arrival at the police station under her real name, Virginia Hall, American citizen, telling them she was a correspondent for the *New York Post* newspaper. As proof, she had already filed a story via Western Union telegram. Headlined BATHROOM OFFICES IN VICHY: REPORTER FINDS CAPITAL CROWDED, the article was ostensibly about how the Vichy government was taking over every available space in its new hometown, including putting offices in hotel bathrooms. Virginia also reported on the lack of taxis and on how her ration book allowed her only ten ounces of meat a week and ten ounces of bread a day, with no rice, spaghetti, or chocolate. "I haven't yet seen any butter, and there is little milk . . . [and] women are no longer entitled to buy cigarettes."

The publication of the article was cause for an outbreak of joy at SOE headquarters. The snippets of information in the article were nuggets of gold as SOE prepared to infiltrate more agents into France. Such local knowledge would allow secret agents to blend in with the crowd, which could mean the difference between life and death. For example, one man had gotten into trouble because he hadn't known that French cafés were only allowed to sell alcohol every other day. His ignorance immediately marked him as an impostor, and he had to run for his life when the café owner called the police.

Virginia's status as a journalist was her sole protection against both the Vichy authorities and the notoriously brutal Nazi secret police, the Gestapo, who were constantly on the lookout for Allied spies, even in the so-called Free Zone in France. Because of this, her priority in her first few days in Vichy was to establish her cover as a journalist. Using her genuine love of France, she met with senior Vichy bureaucrats and policemen, and by appealing to their patriotism, soon had them eating out of her hand. As one historian noted, "She seems to have totally bewitched everybody who knew her."

Some even risked their lives to help her. Suzanne Bertillon, chief censor of the foreign press in Vichy's Ministry of Information, was one person who went out of her way to help. There was something about Virginia that earned Bertillon's trust, and the two became friends. Bertillon not only did not censor Virginia's articles, but she also set up a network of ninety contacts across France (including mayors, farmers, and factory owners) to supply Virginia with information that would prove vital for the British war

An undated portrait of Virginia.

effort. Virginia was able to collect intelligence on the location of ammunition and fuel depots, German troop movements, industrial production, and a German submarine base that was later destroyed by Allied bombs.

In those early days, despite her success in recruiting key helpers, Virginia faced formidable obstacles. Vichy was too small a town to try to lead the double life of a spy disguised as a reporter. She discovered with dismay that there was little interest from the locals in forming a resistance, but plenty of interest in reporting Allied sympathizers to the police, often in exchange for money.

Throughout France, Pétain was a revered hero of World War I. When he shook Adolf Hitler's hand and established his Nazi-sympathizing government, many people were led to believe that it was wrong to resist the German occupation. After a month in Vichy, Virginia moved to the larger city of Lyon, seventy miles to the southeast, in the hope of finding more fertile ground for her work.

Lyon had a tradition of rebelling against authority. Its craft guilds stood up to the clergy in the thirteenth century, and during the French Revolution of 1789, its citizens held out against the Jacobin revolutionaries in Paris. Word reached Virginia that a few uncommonly tough citizens were gathering in the city's smoke-filled bistros and plotting resistance. They "preferred death to German domination." More than a million French prisoners of war—husbands, sons, and brothers—had still not returned home after the fighting at the start of the war, and this was the cause of a quiet but seething anger. French Communists were furious that Germany had broken a peace agreement with Stalin and had invaded the Soviet Union in June 1941. The assassination of a German officer in Nantes had been avenged with the execution of forty-eight French citizens, and these shootings galvanized public opinion in the city against the Nazis and their Vichy supporters.

Lyon was set at the convergence of two major rivers, the Rhône and the Saône, and bounded by two large hills. This dramatic topography, and the city's confusing layout, made it the ideal home for an underground movement. The oldest part of the city was a maze of *traboules*, covered passageways that wove through buildings and streets. Only the locals truly knew their way around them. On the eastern outskirts of town, the flat floodplains of the river Rhône were ideal for parachute drops of agents and supplies.

When Virginia arrived in Lyon, her first and most pressing concern was finding somewhere to stay. The city was thronged with refugees escaping German persecution in occupied France—Lyon being in France's Free Zone—and every hotel and guesthouse was full. There were no apartments available to rent, and she had no friends in the city to turn to.

Exhausted, and by now quite desperate, she dragged herself up the hill above the river Saône to knock on the doors of the St. Elizabeth convent. Fortunately, the sisters took pity on her and gave her a bed in a tiny tower room, where she had the "undivided attention of a strong north wind." The nuns, who wore a "quaint headdress—a white dutch cap with wings," were Virginia's first recruits in Lyon, and SOE had found itself one of the best safe houses in Vichy France, the first of many Virginia was to set up.

As soon as she was able, however, Virginia checked into a hotel in the center of town, using the name "Brigitte Lecontre." To do so, she used fake identity documents created by a forger in London (one of SOE's criminal contacts), which had been battered and stamped on until they looked appropriately worn out. The hotel was an ideal command post. It was close to the US consulate and had several exits—important for a quick getaway—as well as easy access to the tram.

As "Virginia," she made herself known at the US consulate, visiting almost every day in her role as a correspondent from the *New York Post*. Gone was the red hair of Vichy's Miss Hall. She had learned to become less conspicuous, dyeing her hair light brown and drawing it tightly into a bun. Gone too was her chic Parisian wardrobe, including her beloved trousers, abandoned in favor of conservative tweed skirt suits. The freedoms of prewar France and the 1920s Jazz Age had been revoked, and women now dressed modestly to avoid attracting the attention of the French police and their German masters.

Virginia altered her appearance often, depending on who she was meeting. She changed her hairstyle or her makeup, or wore a wide-brimmed hat, glasses, or gloves. She even put slivers of rubber into her mouth to puff out her cheeks. With a little ingenuity, she could be four different women in the space of an afternoon: Brigitte, Virginia, Marie, Germaine.

At the US consulate, the vice consul in Lyon, George Whittinghill, received her warmly. In his official capacity as a diplomat, he had to appear to be neutral, but Virginia quickly and correctly assessed his sympathies, and recruited him as one of her most important helpers. It was not long before they had set up a dependable method of smuggling her messages out of France to the US embassy in Bern, Switzerland: the diplomatic pouch. This was a sealed and clearly labeled bag used by embassies worldwide to transport mail that was legally protected from interference by the host state.

From Bern, the embassy's military expert, Colonel Barnwell Legge, sent them on to London. He forwarded replies and cash back to Lyon in sealed envelopes marked "Marie c/o Lion"—Lion being Whittinghill's code name. Virginia now had a reliable—if slow—channel of communication with SOE. What she really needed was her own radio operator to send and receive messages directly. It would be virtually impossible to organize parachute drops of vital supplies of guns, bullets, and explosives without one.

Although officially just a liaison officer tasked with assisting other agents, Virginia embarked on setting up her own network, code-named Heckler. She needed couriers to carry messages, money, and arms, she needed many safe houses to hide incoming agents and outgoing escapees, and she needed "letter boxes"—people who would take delivery of secret parcels and messages without asking questions. She also needed false identity papers, driving permits, and ration cards—which had to be either produced by specialists recruited locally or sent in from London via the diplomatic pouch—and she needed them fast.

Those she recruited would have to be patient about just how much they could do, however. Their role at this point was mostly simply to exist, to form a secret army that would eventually rise up to attack the Germans when (and not before) the Allies returned to France. It was vital to have everything in place for when the call for action came—but to act too soon would cost lives and alert the enemy. So all assassinations or acts of sabotage that could be attributed to "deliberate interference" were strictly forbidden by SOE command in London. "Fires might mysteriously light themselves," engine bearings might "run hot," or a German car might seize up from sugar in the tank. But things must not "go bang in the night."

CHAPTER 5

NETWORK OF DANGER

Those early days in Lyon were extremely tough for Virginia. An indiscreet word or a momentary lapse might bring her activities to the notice of the Gestapo, who would arrest her on the merest suspicion of working for the Allies. She desperately needed some safe introductions to get her networks going. A list of nine names provided by SOE before her departure proved neither safe nor sufficient, because there was no way of knowing if the people listed were loyal and trustworthy.

September 1941 was a busy month for SOE, which was rapidly gearing up its operations in France. Virginia was impatient to make contact with the dozen or so SOE officers who were now entering France by parachute or boat via the Mediterranean coast. Among the jumpers who arrived on the night of September 6 were George Langelaan, a former *New York Times* correspondent; Michael Trotobas, a charismatic young chef; Vic Gerson, a textiles businessman; and a supremely brave Lancashire engineer, Ben Cowburn. On September 19, several more SOE men arrived on board a converted freighter, including Georges Duboudin (code name: Alain), who headed to Lyon to join Virginia, and Francis Basin (code name: Olive), who remained on the French Riviera.

When SOE agent Gilbert Turck (code name: Christophe) issued an invitation to all his fellow agents across southern France to meet at the Villa des Bois safe house in Marseille, blatantly ignoring basic security rules, gut instinct prevented Virginia from going. Many of the men responded, however. Some went to Marseille for moral support, finding it even tougher in the field than they had expected. Others were so short of money they were virtually starving and went to pick up cash from a recent parachute drop so they could buy food.

Those agents who did go were pounced on by officers of the Sûreté, Vichy's fearsome police force specializing in counterespionage. As a result, the Sûreté practically cleaned out the SOE operation in the whole of the Free Zone. Virtually all SOE's agents and both its Free Zone radio operators were put behind bars and faced the prospect of weeks of torture followed by execution. Most had not yet even started their secret work.

SOE's F Section entered what was seen as a "dark age." After fifteen months of intense recruitment, training, and, finally, infiltration of nearly two dozen agents into France, SOE was left "with little else in the field except Miss Virginia Hall." Only she had a growing network unaffected by the arrests. Only she was supplying vital information on Vichy and the German occupiers. The future of Allied intelligence in France now rested on the shoulders of a single woman.

SOE could count on one hand its remaining officers in the Free Zone: Philippe de Vomécourt (code name: Gauthier), who had been recruited by his brother Pierre; Olive, who was on the Riviera; and Alain, who was in Lyon with Virginia. It was a skeleton operation, and they all depended on Virginia. She alone had the sole reliable means of communicating with London. There was barely an hour in the day when she was not working to make up lost ground.

Just as Vichy and German brutality began to drive more and more French people to consider joining the Resistance, the entire network was in danger of being snuffed out. The Vichy authorities helped the Nazis to round up anyone in France suspected of harboring pro-Resistance views—proving that the Free Zone was not in reality "free" at all. Many dissidents made it too easy. To Virginia's horror, some Resistance fighters needlessly put themselves and others in danger by meeting openly in public and loudly discussing politics. They did not check out new recruits, used their own identities rather than code names, and got into fights with rival Resistance groups. They even wore fur-trimmed war jackets and sunglasses, which was the unofficial Resistance uniform and immediately identified them. When it came to recruiting her own people, Virginia set out to design a much more secure and disciplined system of small groups of handpicked members, all prepared to follow her orders.

Because it had become a hotbed of Resistance activity, Lyon was being closely watched by the Gestapo and the Abwehr (the German military intelligence service). The two German organizations, which were in fact rivals, leaned on the Vichy government and police to do more to crack down on the underground through raids, arrests, and torture.

Most people lived in fear of their neighbors informing on them, and were terrified to open their mouths or break the law. Virginia was disappointed that so few thought it their duty to try to free their country—but perhaps it was hardly surprising. What was the point of risking torture and death in pursuit of what must have seemed like a lost cause to most ordinary French people? Fake news pumped out by Vichy and the Nazis had led many French citizens to believe that there was no future other than under Nazi rule. Some even believed that Britain—which under Prime Minister Winston Churchill had vowed to fight on—had in fact also surrendered.

After centuries of war between Britain and France, many French people already viewed Britain as specifically anti-French. German propaganda took advantage of this ancient distrust by constantly spreading stories that a British blockade was the chief cause of shortages of food, wine, and fuel. Virginia knew that this was a lie. The Germans were stripping France of much of its coal and a large part of its produce—meat, vegetables, fruit, and fish—for their own consumption.

For this reason, she sought instructions from London about

how to spoil food bound for Germany. She was advised to insert "a small piece of putrefied meat" in a carcass, to make a pinhole in tinned provisions, to place salt water in sugar, and to allow vegetables and cereal to get damp. Meanwhile, in one of the articles Virginia wrote for the *New York Post*, she reported that desperate French people were snatching food out of shopping baskets and tearing down fences for firewood. Scrawny pigeons were prized for their meat, as were rabbits, which were sometimes specially bred for food on apartment balconies.

People weighed, on average, fourteen pounds less than before the war, and many had lost teeth and nails to malnutrition. Children were so underfed that their growth was stunted, and many died from common illnesses. Poor diet led to several epidemics, including scarlet fever, diphtheria, and tuberculosis. Virginia herself could scarcely afford to lose any more weight. As winter approached, everyone's health was made even worse by the intense cold. Clothes were scarce, and stocks of leather had been requisitioned by the German military, so there was also a shortage of shoes.

It was hardly fertile ground for creating an underground network, but Virginia had luck when the vice consul at the US consulate, George Whittinghill, introduced her to William Simpson, a British Royal Air Force (RAF) pilot who visited him almost every day at the consulate. Shot down in flames over Belgium in May 1940, Simpson had spent months recuperating, wrapped in greased bandages for his burns, and was now awaiting repatriation to Britain. His once-handsome face was terribly scarred, part of his nose and left eyelid were missing, and some of his fingers had been amputated. His left foot and knee were also badly affected, and he limped painfully.

Having both suffered life-altering injuries, Simpson and Virginia developed an instant rapport, and he went out of his way to help her, while also grasping the opportunity to feel useful again. He introduced Virginia to Germaine Guérin, one of Lyon's most celebrated residents, who was secretly doing everything she could to fight the Germans.

Germaine was nobody's idea of a typical Resistance fighter. She welcomed German officers, French police, Vichy officials, and wealthy businessmen into her house, supplying them with smuggled Scotch whisky, prime beef steaks, and the company of the prostitutes who worked for her—all at exorbitant prices. In return, her clients provided her with otherwise unobtainable gasoline—never suspecting she was using her car to transport secret agents and escapees—and coal, an almost impossible luxury that freezing winter of 1941.

From the outside, Germaine's home looked scruffy and unkempt, but inside it was a treasure house of tapestries, wooden chests full of gold coins, and wardrobes stuffed with Parisian couture. She draped herself in jewels, silks, and furs, and was usually surrounded by black cats. One of her kittens was known for following her devotedly down the street. Her lifestyle was all funded by the business downstairs.

When Virginia and Germaine met for the first time, both

women were wary of each other. The Frenchwoman was proud and fiercely patriotic. She instinctively balked at joining a formal Resistance network and especially at the idea of taking orders from a foreigner. But she was won over by Virginia's evident integrity and courage, and became a pillar of Virginia's entire Lyon operation and one of its most heroic agents. She became a "rallying point" for many SOE agents coming through Lyon, as well as Jews fleeing the Occupied Zone, Poles on their way to fight, and refugees making their way south to Spain. She found them somewhere to hide, supplied them with food, clothes, and false papers, and sent them on their way to freedom.

Virginia's recruitment of Germaine marked an entirely new stage in her mission. Her Heckler network was now viewed by SOE as "solidly established," with a roster of exceptionally useful and committed recruits, at the center of which was this unlikely pair of women.

Germaine's powers over well-placed Frenchmen opened all sorts of doors. A wealthy engineer named Eugène Jeunet, a widower with three children, had a valuable pass to cross the demarcation line between the two French zones. He offered to shuttle Virginia's messages to and from underground groups in Paris, which gave her the chance to extend her network far beyond her Lyon base. He also provided transport, gasoline, accommodation, and food, and hid arms, explosives, and radios at his workplace.

By lucky coincidence, Jeunet's brother-in-law was the local

chief of police. He agreed not to look too closely into what Virginia was doing, and to tip her off when his officers were about to mount a raid or make an arrest. His well-timed warnings protected her from capture many times, and also saved a number of her most important agents.

Germaine's women took the biggest risks to provide Virginia with intelligence. They plied their clients with alcohol to loosen their tongues, and when the men were asleep, they rifled through their pockets for papers that might be of interest to the Resistance, and took photographs of them. They even risked putting itching powder into the men's clothes to cause them discomfort and keep them from working. While once Virginia had nothing but contempt for prostitutes who entertained German clients, now she affectionately dubbed such women her "tart friends." Thanks to them, she knew "a hell of a lot!" about the German war effort, information that she swiftly passed straight back to London.

Germaine also introduced Virginia to Dr. Jean Rousset, a jolly figure with a rakish mustache. Rousset already sheltered Jews and escaped prisoners of war, and his doctor's office concealed piles of Resistance pamphlets. He had been waiting for the chance to do more for the Allied cause. Now, at last, here was someone who could organize the Resistance and supply them with outside help.

Virginia liked Rousset's optimism, energy, and vast network of similarly minded friends. She code-named him Pépin, meaning "pip" or "seed," and made him her right-hand man. Like so many others before and after, Rousset was bowled over by Virginia's force of character. Her authority, competence, and charisma were obvious, but so too was her selflessness.

Vice consul George Whittinghill also joined Virginia's efforts, and spent his own money on many occasions to help RAF pilots and British and Belgian agents escape to Spain. British airmen were advised that if they were shot down in France they should head for the US consulate in Lyon and declare themselves to be "a friend of Olivier." This was the password that meant they wanted to be put in touch with Virginia. Word began circulating far and wide of the miracle-working Marie Monin (another of Virginia's code names).

As liaison officer, Virginia's orders were to coordinate (rather than lead) different networks of agents, but SOE's desperation for progress, combined with her ability to inspire and unite many French people from all sorts of backgrounds, saw her going way beyond her original job description. She recruited a scent manufacturer, Joseph Marchand, who provided a safe house in Lyon for agents and went on to head one of her networks; a pair of elderly sisters, the Mesdemoiselles Fellot, whose antique shop hid supplies and whose apartment sheltered agents on the run from the Nazis and the Vichy police; the owner of a lingerie shop, France Pejot, who stored weapons under piles of lacy bras and hosted meetings in her back room; and several hairdressers who helped Resistance fighters change their appearance when they needed to.

Another of Virginia's recruits, Madame Alberte, took in messages at her laundry, signaling that there was something to collect by placing two stockings close together in the window. If the stockings were far apart, nothing had come in. Virginia also recruited a forger, Monsieur Chambrillard, who created official papers that fooled even the most eagle-eyed inspectors. Many others—factory foremen, railway workers, police officers, government officials, and housewives—plucked up the courage to approach the attractive woman with the strong accent and offer her help. Everyone who worked for her knew that if they were caught, the penalty would be torture and death.

Virginia traveled extensively, leaving no potentially useful contact untapped. Through a combination of personal recommendations and carefully judged approaches to strangers, she enlisted more and more recruits. By giving away some of her own feelings about the war, and her burning desire for a free France, she had a way of making people warm to her. But she also made it clear that only by joining an SOE-approved network and following her orders could they be guaranteed deliveries of arms, explosives, food, money, and medicine. SOE could and would provide supplies, but her recruits had to keep their side of the bargain.

Perhaps her biggest achievement was infiltrating the dreaded Sûreté, the Vichy government's counterespionage force. Virginia identified and recruited one of the Sûreté's officers, Marcel Leccia, and then, incredibly, both his assistant (Elisée Allard) and boss (Léon Guth). Now she would be warned of future traps like the one at the safe house in Marseille that had netted them so many SOE agents, and she could reasonably hope that the Sûreté would be lenient with any of her people that they did manage to arrest.

CHAPTER 6

MARIE THE BRAVE

As winter set in, the constant traveling through sleet, snow, and slush became arduous, and, in Virginia's own words, a "grim undertaking not to be embarked upon lightly. It is devastating for the weak and exhausting even for the strong." Her roaming about the country was incredibly risky. Trains were subject to surprise police inspections, sometimes attended by the much-feared Gestapo.

The safest option while traveling was to keep incriminating papers (containing messages too long to commit to memory, or perhaps technical details of potential sabotage targets) in one hand. This meant they could easily be pushed down between the seat cushions, thrown out onto the track, or even eaten if necessary. Some agents held up tiny mirrors at each station to be able to see who was about to board the train behind them, so they could be prepared for approaching trouble.

Virginia noticed that the police took more interest in the cheaper carriages, so she made sure always to travel in first class.

In addition, she memorized the address of where she was going rather than writing it down, and always had a plausible reason for her journey worked out and rehearsed. Even so, every trip put her in mortal danger—and her prosthetic leg meant that she could not jump from the train and run for cover.

That winter, the outside temperature plummeted to five degrees Fahrenheit. Virginia's unheated hotel room was not much warmer. She blocked the drafts from the windows with old rags and lined her clothes with newspaper, which rustled when she moved. Far worse was the wartime shortage of soap: she had none for washing either herself or her clothes and sheets. "If you could ever send me a piece of soap," she wrote to London via the diplomatic pouch, "I should be both very happy and much cleaner." The biggest challenge of all was running out of the special socks that cushioned her stump from Cuthbert.

For Virginia, since losing her leg, rigid self-reliance had become second nature. She was doing important work, and doing it well. She had a role, a purpose. Although she was terrified, and lonely, and although capture was a real prospect every minute of every day, she had never felt so free.

So great was Virginia's success that Marie Monin was fast becoming known far beyond the city of Lyon. The bar at the Grand Nouvel Hôtel, which she visited most evenings at six, was known across France and beyond as the place for agents to go for money, refuge, false papers, or help escaping to Spain. Virginia also supplied new arrivals with food, tobacco, clothes, and shoes. She was probably too willing to help others, even though—or perhaps because—there had been no one to give such support to her. She took great joy in being valued.

New agents were better prepared than Virginia had been. Since the arrests in Marseille, greater attention was given to false names and identities, perfect French, and security training, in part thanks to Virginia's critical reports. Yet most still felt uncomfortably conspicuous in their first days. "You almost imagine that neon lights are blinking from your forehead and proclaiming, on and off, 'Made in England,'" recalled Peter Churchill, a thirty-two-year-old former ice hockey player who left London in December 1941 to travel to the south of France by submarine.

Virginia reminded newcomers that trivial errors could cost them their lives. They should remember to eat like Frenchmen—using bread to wipe up their gravy, not leaving a speck of food on the plate, and certainly not lining up their cutlery neatly when they finished eating. Another easy mistake was forgetting that the French drove on the opposite side of the road from the British. One agent was caught by a keen-eyed Gestapo officer after looking the wrong way and walking out in front of a car.

SOE considered Virginia "amazingly successful" and rated her work and field craft as "inspired." But not everyone was pleased. Alain, one of the few other SOE agents who had avoided the Sûreté trap at the Villa des Bois in Marseille, was in Lyon with Virginia, and he was her superior in rank. Alain was jealous that a woman who was a mere liaison officer—and a woman with a disability at that—was proving much better at the job than he was. He presumed a natural superiority over her.

Yet when Virginia had introduced Alain to a local Resistance group on his arrival in Lyon, he had failed to turn up at meetings, and seemed incapable of recruiting many helpers to his network—or of keeping those he did. He boasted to SOE that he had enlisted ten thousand men, but Virginia knew that the truth was more like only a handful. She saw that he was becoming unhinged by the strains of his undercover life and the hyperalert isolation it demanded.

Worried that he was becoming a major security risk, Virginia refused to give him access to her own network, let alone take it over. She saw her people as her responsibility. They trusted her and her alone. Having lost most of her fellow agents at the Villa des Bois, she knew well the danger of a weak link in the chain. And her missing leg was a constant reminder of the terrible price of carelessness. She kept her contacts in separate groups who knew little about each other, or about her (beyond one of her code names), and insisted they keep in touch only by leaving messages at a safe location, such as Madame Alberte's laundry. When SOE suggested that Alain take command of her recruits, she told them to "lay off."

Peter Churchill returned to England after his mission in France and told SOE about Virginia's frustration with Alain. Churchill described Alain as a bully and suggested he be recalled to London before he caused any more problems. Alain's irresponsible conduct was putting Virginia in danger, and losing her could be even more damaging to the cause than the disastrous arrests at the Villa des Bois. Churchill could not have been more complimentary about Virginia, and he proposed that SOE make her life easier—and reflect reality on the ground—by officially putting her in charge. She "knows everyone," he said, "is in with everyone, liked by everyone."

But formalizing a woman's position as chief or giving her clear authority to take command in the field was a step too far, even for SOE. It seemed that no matter what Virginia had achieved in establishing SOE's only solid foothold in France, and no matter how unsubstantiated Alain's claims about his own progress turned out to be, his word was taken more seriously in London than hers. There was even growing irritation in SOE at Virginia's refusal to take orders from Alain or to hand over her network to his control.

Peter Churchill's mission in France had been to investigate what had happened to the agents arrested at the Villa des Bois raid in Marseille. But it was Virginia whose contacts found out that the men were being held in Périgueux jail in southwest France. This was the first firm indication in three long months that the captured agents were still alive. Without the human rights protections guaranteed to regular fighting forces by international law, secret agents were unlikely to survive capture. Of the 119 London-based SOE agents arrested in France during the entire war, only fifteen, or one in eight, came home.

Mauzac prison camp, southwest France.

Now at last there was hope that a plan could be hatched to rescue at least some of SOE's finest agents. Churchill and Virginia had arranged to meet in Marseille to exchange information before he headed back to England.

Just before their rendezvous, she had another meeting with SOE agent Olive in a nearby café. As Virginia and Olive were getting ready to leave the café, there was a commotion: the shrill shrieking of police whistles and screaming and shouting. Dozens of armed policemen ran into the café and ordered the customers to line up against the wall.

The Vichy government had tried to recruit thousands of workers to send to Germany, telling lies about the good food, pay, and free vacations on offer, but few had been fooled, and the numbers had fallen far short of Nazi demands. Now police were rounding up innocent people at random to provide Hitler with slave labor.

To escape the roundups, young men disappeared into the *maquis*, the dense mountain undergrowth typical of the southern French countryside. "Taking to the *maquis*" became a common phrase across most of France. At first it meant running off to hide in the wild terrain, but it came to refer to bands of dissidents—*maquisards*—and their Resistance groups.

Now Vichy officials had agreed to forced deportations to placate their Nazi masters, and Marseille was one of the cities targeted. If they didn't have three hundred workers on their way to Germany within three days, their own policemen would be put on the trains instead.

Virginia and Olive were in the wrong place at the wrong time. The police had blocked off the entire street, and there was no way they could escape. Virginia was frantically trying to think of a way out when the district police commissioner marched in to scrutinize his captives, many of whom were beginning to cry. An inspector followed the commissioner in, at which point Olive linked arms with Virginia. She thought he was trying to comfort her, but actually it was a signal from the quick-thinking Olive to the inspector that they were together. The inspector pointed to them and ordered one of his men to lock them into a back room, saying he would deal with them "privately."

A few streets away, Peter Churchill was surprised and disappointed that Virginia was not at the café as she had promised. It was not like her to be late, and he always felt safer when she was around. He sat down facing the door and ordered a drink, then pretended to read a newspaper. He wondered why the place was empty and could sense tension in the air.

Virginia heard the door lock behind her and Olive, and she thought their fate was sealed, but the room contained a small window that opened onto an alleyway. While the other customers were shoved screaming into trucks at the front of the building, they climbed up and squeezed through the narrow opening, one after the other. Virginia looped her good leg over the ledge and pulled Cuthbert through, then eased herself down on the other side. They scrabbled to get away and find Churchill.

When they found him at the café, Olive took Churchill's arm and quietly said, "Let's go." Churchill knew that something must be very wrong. He threw his payment down onto the table and followed. "They're raiding the cafés," Olive explained as he led Churchill and Virginia up a flight of stairs to a safe flat. Then he told them both, with a grin, that the police inspector who had sent them to the back room was an old friend. He had deliberately given them the chance to escape.

Their instinct was to get out of town right away, but Virginia advised waiting until the morning. More roundups were likely to take place, and the train station would be a "humming hive of hatred." Suddenly crushed by the dangers confronting him, Churchill felt more in awe of Virginia than ever. Perhaps it was his vulnerable state that prompted a rare moment of softness in Virginia during those anxious hours at the safe house. She admitted to him that she felt “a hundred years old” from facing fear all the time.

“When you get home, it’ll look different from a distance,” she said with a smile. “You’ll forget how cold you were—except to bring warmer clothes next time. You’ll forget all the frights you’ve had, and you’ll only remember the excitement.”

CHAPTER 7

EXPOSED

On December 7, 1941, Japanese bombers attacked the US navy base at Pearl Harbor, near Honolulu, Hawaii, killing more than twenty-four hundred Americans. The United States declared war against Japan the next day, which brought it crashing into the conflict against Germany and Italy, on the same side as the British and Russians.

Virginia's boss at the *New York Post*, George Backer, sent her a telegram, urging her to return to the United States. As an American, she was in far greater danger now that her country was at war, and Backer thought she should reconsider her mission. Her journalist cover would now offer little if any protection.

Virginia refused to leave.

Yet the start of 1942 saw her in an uncharacteristically gloomy state of mind. Since the attack on Pearl Harbor, all communications from her family had stopped, apart from one telegram from her mother at Christmas, which had been passed through the normal diplomatic route by SOE. A homemade fruitcake sent by Mrs.

Hall didn't arrive. "We never despair," Virginia wrote to Nicolas Bodington on January 5, "but . . . it seems unfair."

Lonely, and no doubt fearful, she let down her guard in an acutely personal letter to "My dear Nic," typewritten on her bed while sleet flecked the windows of her hotel room. Despite her determination to stay in France, she confessed that her health was suffering. She had a cold and an "ache in the thorax" caused by the persistent "snow, rain and slush . . . The dark days are fairly abysmal."

"I get so 'fed up,'" she sighed, pleading with SOE staffers to write to her in the absence of any letters from her family at home. "I resent this dearth of mail, and this barren desert in which I exist. Gosh, and gosh durn, I do!" She ended, though, with a typically upbeat note: She would "get over it." She sent her love to the office and signed off with "Cheers, Dindy."

The harsh winter meant that no new agents, let alone radio operators, had been dropped into France. Daytime flights from Britain were too dangerous, and because pilots relied on moonlight to identify landmarks such as lakes or hills to navigate their route, there were only a handful of opportunities for flying missions each month, which were easily lost to bad weather.

The F Section of SOE was thus still dependent on Virginia's slow message route via the US consulate to communicate with its agents. SOE agent Lucas, who was based in Paris in the Occupied Zone, decided that the situation was intolerable and set out to find a radio operator somehow. He believed there must have been

SOE agent Ben Cowburn

someone transmitting to Britain independent of SOE, and he made it his business to find them.

For Virginia, the first sign of trouble came late one afternoon in February when an unshaven figure in filthy clothes came knocking frantically on her door. It was SOE agent Ben Cowburn, who Virginia knew from his previous missions to France—she rated him SOE's most brilliant agent. He was clearly exhausted and starving, and she quickly ushered him in before he attracted unwanted attention.

Cowburn told Virginia that she was in great danger. Her existence and whereabouts were most likely known to the Germans, and it was only a matter of time before they came for her. He pleaded with her to leave Lyon at once. After all, she had already been in France for six months, and that was normally considered the limit of any mission. Cowburn himself kept his time in the field short to avoid detection or excessive fatigue.

Instead of panicking, Virginia arranged for Cowburn to have his first bath in a week and a clean pair of pajamas. Then she sent word to her contacts in Marseille to organize his escape over the Pyrenees into Spain. She would make up her mind about her own situation when she had heard the full story. Her composure at this moment astonished Cowburn. It seemed the greater the peril she faced, the more calmer and more resolute she became.

He told her how, several weeks earlier, on December 26, SOE agent Lucas had met with a dark-haired Frenchwoman named Mathilde Carré, nicknamed La Chatte (the Cat) for her unusual green eyes, in a café on the Champs-Élysées in Paris. He desperately hoped that the rumors she had access to a radio were true. Wearing her trademark red hat, La Chatte confirmed that she had a radio, and offered to send a message to London on Lucas's behalf.

Both Lucas and SOE were delighted to have established direct radio contact. But, seduced by La Chatte's charms, Lucas had not asked enough questions. In fact, Carré was romantically involved and living with a man named Hugo Bleicher, who was a member of the German military intelligence service, the Abwehr. She was passing all of Lucas's radio messages to and from SOE to him.

Thanks to the intercepted messages, Bleicher was able to piece together details about Lucas's Resistance network in France, including new arrivals of agents. He was particularly intrigued by someone operating in the area around Lyon. Whoever this "man" was, he was clearly the lynchpin of Allied intelligence. As a result of Bleicher's investigations, this Lyon network was now regarded by German high command in Berlin as the "number one enemy" to internal security, and its leader needed to be tracked down and eliminated. By the time Lucas became suspicious of La Chatte, a couple of weeks later, the damage was done: Bleicher had compiled a list of key names and addresses.

Cowburn knew he had a duty to warn Virginia before it was too late. Like Peter Churchill, he recognized that her loss to SOE would be a calamity. No one else had her contacts, her communication route, or her skills and resolve. He also had to find a way to inform SOE that the radio was in German hands, and that they must stop using it and stop sending more agents to a near certain death. After an epic journey across France over five nights of nail-biting tension, Cowburn arrived in Vichy. He dashed past the Gestapo surveillance team into the US embassy to beg them to wire London with the news. Then he traveled on to Lyon to warn Virginia.

Despite his pleas and the mounting dangers, Virginia decided to stay put. The fact that the Nazis were onto her made her even more determined to prove her ability by evading them. The French were "still hoping for their victory and many, many of them are willing to help," she noted. There were some small signs of hope, including indications of resistance where before there had been cooperation. Factory workers were slowing down production by striking in protest at the lack of food and fuel, by losing important documents, and by switching labels on goods. More and more police were changing sides and passing on information.

Dr. Rousset and Germaine continued to work tirelessly for Virginia, recruiting helpers and finding safe houses. Rousset's popularity extended far and wide, and a request from him was something most people were eager to oblige. Indeed, "I've come on behalf of the doctor" became a standard SOE password in much of southern France. Together with Virginia, the trio formed a permanent framework for SOE that spawned several new networks reaching south to the coast, east to the Swiss border, and north to Paris. Virginia could now call on the support of hundreds of men and women across France in dozens of professions.

Even though Virginia took what Maurice Buckmaster, the head of SOE's F Section and Bodington's boss, described as "insane and incredible" risks by recruiting so many different people to the cause, she was no fool. She changed her field name from Marie to Isabelle to Philomène. She varied her routes home, checked constantly that she was not being followed, and never approached a house or a café without walking around the block first. She avoided going to the same place every day and altered her appearance frequently. She also acquired a French driver's license so she didn't have to take so many trains.

Yet the risks of betrayal and infiltration were mounting, and her luck, spycraft, and police protectors could not hold out forever. One evening, a young man turned up at her door claiming to be an SOE parachutist. He was persistent, and in some ways plausible, but Virginia's instincts made her suspicious. Feigning ignorance, she turned him away. It was a close call. She heard soon after that a number of Nazi agents were trying to infiltrate themselves into her network.

Hugo Bleicher's interest in a shadowy figure in Lyon had come to the notice of the Gestapo, and the Abwehr and Gestapo were now competing to hunt down the notorious agent they knew to be somewhere in the city. Bleicher was unusual in being a cultured figure who liked to outwit his enemies rather than bludgeon them. The Gestapo's preferred method for getting information, by contrast, was torture.

Sensing the mounting danger, Virginia stepped up her security. She moved to a three-room apartment in an elegant square of solid six-story houses. Her corner building, no. 3 place Ollier, had several useful exits, including a discreet doorway at the back. When there was a flowerpot behind the ornamental ironwork at her front window, it meant it was safe to knock on the door.

Cowburn was amazed and concerned by the stream of people who came to the apartment asking for Virginia's help, like she was some sort of fairy godmother. She supplied them with contacts, and also with food, soap, and cash. She even did their laundry for them. Her activism extended to distributing cash to the families of Resistance fighters in prison, as well as arranging for the Red Cross to send food parcels to the captured SOE men in Périgueux jail. When people asked for help, she found the greatest pleasure in being the one able to provide it. "She was paying the price of having a strong, reliable personality: Everybody brought their troubles to her," Cowburn observed.

There was never a dull moment, but that was exactly how Virginia liked it. She was now developing a new line of work: breaking agents out of prison—what she called her "unofficial releases." No one else seemed to be doing it—and it went way beyond her original brief—but she railed at the fact that many of SOE's greatest talents were being left to simply waste away in French jails. Why should she not use her contacts in the French police, hospitals, and prisons? She relished the chance to make a truly significant contribution to the intelligence war, and so she took it.

One of Virginia's earliest successes was orchestrating the escape of a senior SOE agent named Gerry Morel, who was also in Périgueux jail. She enlisted the help of her recruit, Léon Guth, regional chief of the Sûreté in Limoges, a town 250 miles away from Lyon, famous for its porcelain. She and Guth enjoyed "very cordial" relations, and whenever she traveled to his area, she stayed with him and his wife. She called his subordinates, Marcel Leccia and Elisée Allard, her "nephews," and Guth himself her "most special friend."

Virginia told Guth that he had to help her save Morel, and the pair hatched a meticulous plan. Agent Morel deliberately stopped eating, and his health rapidly worsened, almost certainly with assistance from SOE's famous sickness tablets, smuggled in by Virginia. These caused symptoms similar to typhoid: stomach cramps and a high fever. Friendly wardens moved Morel to a prison hospital in Limoges for surgery, and afterward the cooperative guard outside his room obligingly dozed off. Morel crept out of his bed, slipped on a doctor's white coat, and, with the aid of a sympathetic nurse, scaled the hospital perimeter wall.

Another helper was waiting on the far side to provide him with a suit and shoes.

He then traveled through a snowstorm to one of Virginia's safe houses, where he gathered his strength before pushing on to her apartment in Lyon. A few days later, despite the dangers of being caught with Morel, who was by then the target of a major national manhunt, Virginia accompanied him by train to join the escape line she had helped to set up. Dubbed the Vic Line—in honor of its chief, Vic Gerson—the escape route crossed the border from Perpignan, France, into Spain. It would see hundreds of agents and airmen to safety.

Back in London, there was "stupefaction" at Virginia's success, and Morel also marveled at what she had done for him. "Her amazing personality, integrity, and enthusiasm were an example and inspiration for us all," he reported. "No task was too great or too small for her; and whatever she undertook she put into it all her energy, sparing herself nothing." Morel's escape was the first such operation Virginia directed herself. With its success, she proved that she could take charge in spectacular style. And it was just the warm-up act.

CHAPTER 8

A PIANIST AT LAST

Thanks to her vast network of contacts, Virginia heard about the arrival of a radio operator, or "pianist," in Marseille. Donald Dunton (code name: Georges 35) had parachuted in a month earlier, at the end of January 1942, landing twenty-five miles away from the designated spot because of a pilot error. Ever since, he had been wandering around France, trying and failing to make contact with other agents, and now he was looking to return to Britain. Virginia quickly tracked him down, persuaded him to stay, and told him where he could find a working radio. Thanks to her initiative, her agents once again had direct radio communications with London.

Meanwhile, she continued to be held back by some of her SOE colleagues. As an official network chief, it was Alain's responsibility to build up and train groups of men, and to plan for parachute drops of explosives, arms, and ammunition. He gave every impression of activity, bombarding London with talk about his many friends in the police and press, and among the gangsters of Lyon.

SOE believed his stories, and sent him half a million francs to fund his impressive-sounding operations, such as a grandiose plan for blowing up a railway.

Virginia was not one to hold her tongue, and thought it her duty to point out to SOE that actually, in her opinion, Alain was cowardly and lazy. Far from having built up a large, well-trained, and cohesive force, he had simply wasted the intelligence (and volunteers) she was sending him. Despite his claims, he had failed to retain almost all the men Virginia had supplied him—and certainly none who were properly trained or managed.

"A good executive and organizer would be greatly appreciated," she wrote pointedly to Nicolas Bodington in March. She had made so many contacts and had painstakingly researched suitable sabotage targets, "but they need following up and organizing, none of which has been done." With most of the better agents, like Cowburn, only dropping in and out on short missions, and the agents who had been arrested in Marseille still languishing in jail, she was carrying too much of the load on her own.

The other SOE agent in the area, Gauthier, wasn't much use either. SOE later conceded that he, too, was "slapdash" and "most difficult" toward Virginia. Gauthier also made spurious claims about the size of his network (boasting of two thousand men when the truth was more like half a dozen), and failed to look after newly arrived SOE agents. He left one pair waiting in a Lyon café for seventeen days, and they had to spend their nights sleeping in a ditch.

SOE agent Georges Duboudin (code name: Alain)

"We could use about six clever chaps," sighed Virginia, "perfectly and utterly reliable persons—persons from 'home.'"

Perhaps the arrival in Lyon of his own long-awaited wireless operator would galvanize Alain into action. When Edward Zeff, a "man of nerve and resource," arrived by submarine in April, Virginia was overjoyed. Zeff was soon transmitting for as many as six hours a day, organizing drops of arms for Alain's supposedly huge army on designated zones just outside Lyon.

Alain soon received plastic explosives, fuses, detonators, Sten guns, and Colt pistols. There were also cigarettes, chocolate, packets of tea (a favorite comfort of Virginia's), and itching powder (no doubt for Germaine's women). It was an impressive stash, and Alain passed on the munitions to a small band of his favorite underground contacts. He did not, however, share his training in their storage or use, and the guns rusted in damp conditions. The explosives were largely wasted on "irritating acts with no real value," such as blowing up newspaper kiosks.

Virginia raged at what she saw as waste and incompetence, and asked that in the future only properly trained SOE operatives should take receipt of arms and explosives, rather than amateur Resistance fighters unfamiliar with both. But without London's backing, there was nothing she could do. She was still ranked as a mere liaison officer.

Her fury brought the conflict with Alain to a boil. Aware that she had complained about him, Alain sent a message to SOE, accusing Virginia of claiming credit for all his (unspecified) achievements. "I know my job. Marie is of no use to me, and if somebody has to give orders, I shall, not her."

To make matters even more heated, Zeff contacted London to complain about both of them: Alain for lacking leadership and Virginia for being prickly. SOE responded a week later by informing Alain, Zeff, and Virginia that they were all doing first-class work, but that they were not there to squabble.

Zeff was right about Alain, but he may also have had a point about Virginia. It was true that after months in the field, the pressure was taking its toll. As more agents came in, so did other difficult characters. Virginia's position was made all the more challenging by her lack of military rank, making her authority easier to question. Zeff frequently ignored her instructions and constantly demanded more money. Virginia worried that he and other agents were taking advantage by socking away SOE cash for themselves. "What happens to soldiers who refuse to obey orders?" she asked in one dispatch. "What do you recommend for men sent by you who flatly refuse to obey orders received from you? Have I authority to deal with such cases as I see fit?"

• • •

IN JUNE 1942, the US consul, Marshall Vance, was interrogated by the Sûreté as to whether he knew Virginia. He denied categorically that he did, and shortly after, on a visit to Bern, Switzerland, he warned a British MI6 agent there that Virginia was clearly a target and that her "outfit [was] completely compromised." While her own integrity was not in doubt, too many around her had been careless.

Deeply alarmed, SOE informed Virginia that her work was "appreciated," but that it was now time to discuss her future. The curt wording outraged her. She had survived in the field for nine long months. What else could she do to prove that she could handle herself? Surely it was up to her to judge whether or not her security had been compromised? Didn't she have well-placed contacts in the police who protected her?

For all the fear, she had never been so happy. For all the frustration, she had never felt so fulfilled. For all the traitors and collaborators, she still desired more than anything to help the good people of France. She would not meekly obey an order to return to the confines of her old life without a fight.

But she knew she had to be tactical. She delayed her response to the orders, blaming bad atmospheric conditions for making transmitting difficult. Next, she converted a colleague into a powerful ally. Cowburn, who before had pleaded with her to leave, now sent in a report "urging the importance" of her work, emphasizing the "difficulty of passing her connections to others," and insisting that "no one . . . was capable of replacing her."

Virginia promised to scale down her operations, to change apartments, to see only a handful of her most security-minded contacts. For the others, such as Gauthier, she would "cease to exist." It became clear a few days later what she had been working on, and why she did not want to leave.

CHAPTER 9

MISSION IMPOSSIBLE

Périgueux jail was a somber fortress with stinking, damp dungeons. The twelve SOE agents captured by the Sûreté at the Villa des Bois in Marseille had festered there for six months, and morale was low. They had endured a long winter without heat, and were allowed outside for only ten minutes a day. The only tap had frozen solid, and they had been unable to wash.

The men (known as "Clan Cameron" within SOE) were still awaiting trial, and there was no guarantee that they would not be handed over to the Nazis or face a firing squad. Virginia had not forgotten them, and her occasional food parcels had given them some comfort, but she was frustrated she could not do more.

A Frenchman named Jean Pierre-Bloch had been arrested along with the men, and his wife, Gaby Bloch, had been visiting him and trying to drum up support for him on the outside. She had lobbied ministers in Vichy to no avail, and her options were running out. Gaby and the Camerons had lost faith in SOE's sporadic efforts to have them freed, but they had heard about Gerry Morel's escape, and how it had been brought about in large part thanks to the help of the legendary Marie of Lyon.

So Gaby made her way to Lyon to ask for help. Virginia was impressed by the courage of this petite Frenchwoman—all the more so because of the incredible dangers she faced as a Jewish person. French authorities were now obeying Nazi orders to arrest thousands of Jews for deportation to the concentration camps in Poland.

Gaby described the hardships of Périgueux jail: the beatings, the dark, the disease, the daily diet of one bowl of greasy liquid and a tiny crust of bread. She told Virginia how rats would gnaw at the bodies of the ill and the weak, and how everyone was crawling with lice. The Camerons' strength and spirits were plummeting fast. Virginia was their last hope.

Virginia appreciated all too well the scale of the problem. Périgueux jail was an impenetrable stronghold of high walls and iron gates, from which no one ever escaped. She informed SOE, though, that "if they cannot come out officially, they will come out unofficially."

After months of watching others fail, this was a chance for her to prove what she could do. In the absence of any other progress, SOE finally gave Virginia the authority to have a go herself at freeing the men. There seems to have been little faith in London that she would succeed. Using her considerable cunning and ingenuity, Virginia persuaded the US ambassador to France,

Admiral William Leahy, to lobby his friendliest contacts in the Vichy government to move the Camerons to an outdoor prison camp at Mauzac, in southwest France. Conditions there would be considerably better, even though the men's lives still hung in the balance.

She considered springing them during the twenty-five-mile transfer between the two prisons, but learned that after months of maltreatment the men were too weak to make a run for it. Furthermore, they would be in chains for the journey, and the guards had orders to shoot anyone who tried to break free. The operation would have to wait.

Virginia was too well known to be seen near the camp, so three times a week, Gaby Bloch made the seventy-mile round-trip visit to research options for an escape. Sometimes she stayed at the local hotel, where several camp wardens drank at the bar in their free time. Virginia supplied her with plenty of money to buy drinks, and trained her to identify potential helpers without putting herself at unnecessary risk.

Gaby duly chatted in the bar, as casually as possible, just as Virginia had instructed her, about how an Allied victory was a certainty. To anyone who seemed genuinely interested, she would add that there were ways in which victory could be sped up, and that there might be handsome rewards in return. One of the guards, José Sevilla, offered to help, and he turned out to be extremely useful. He persuaded the camp commandant that Watchtower Five—the nearest to the Camerons' hut—should not be guarded at night, claiming convincingly that it swayed in the wind and that its ladder was unsafe in the dark.

Soon afterward, Gaby started taking her husband a supply of clean clothes, books, and large quantities of food on every one of her permitted visits. Virginia gave her money to buy a list of carefully selected black market groceries, so that it looked as if she were merely a devoted wife wanting to feed her husband. But one of the jars of jam concealed a tiny file, and hidden in a pile of fresh laundry was a pair of wire cutters. Hollowed-out books held a small screwdriver and hammer, and tins of sardines in tomato sauce were made of the best possible reusable metal. Gaby's extraordinary courage and Virginia's ingenuity meant that the men soon had all they needed to make a key for the door of the barracks, using bread from the canteen to make a mold of the lock.

At the same time, Virginia was hard at work planning the next stage of the escape. She enlisted Vic Gerson, the chief of the escape line, to find safe houses and to organize the Camerons' eventual passage over the Pyrenees to Spain. Together they recruited a getaway driver and arranged papers, ration cards, and train tickets. Most important, they found a hideaway not too far from the camp for those nail-biting first hours and days when the danger of recapture was at its highest. There were countless details to arrange, requiring all of Virginia's field skills and resourcefulness. The escape mission was the main reason she had been so dismayed when she received recall orders from London.

Gaby's visits and Sevilla's help were not enough for the men to finalize their plans. SOE needed a quick way of contacting them inside the camp. They came up with a breathtaking solution. One sunny morning, an elderly French priest, a jovial army veteran who had lost his legs in World War I, started a series of pastoral visits to the Camerons. He was good at lifting their morale, and arranged for the men to be allowed a few cans of paint to spruce up their hut.

When they finished the decorating, he asked them to lift his wheelchair up the steps and into their barracks so he could see their work. Once inside, he beckoned the men to gather round. "I have a little present for you," he whispered, his eyes darting excitedly around at them. "First, post a sentry or two at the door and window . . . Now, one of you look under my cassock . . . where my legs should be."

One of them duly lifted up the robe, and there was a collective gasp as a radio was revealed. "Great Scott! It's a piano!" exclaimed Georges Bégué upon seeing it.

"Yes," the priest replied. "I was given to understand that you can get plenty of music out of it . . . Hide it and, of course, forget how it got here."

Within a week, Bégué had transmitted his first message to SOE. F Section was astonished to hear from its celebrated pianist from inside a French prison camp. Bégué sent so many messages that the signal attracted the attention of a Gestapo radio-detector van, which was seen passing the camp on at least one occasion. But he was confident that the police would never think to look inside the camp, and he was right.

Shortly after four in the afternoon on July 15, the last possible day in the lunar cycle when it would be fully dark at night, the men waited for the signal from Virginia that all was ready. Sure enough, an old lady passed by the camp at the appointed time with three children in her wake. If it had been an old man, that would have meant that the operation had been called off.

At around midnight, Sevilla started a drinking session in the guardroom. As soon as the guards had relaxed and started singing, it had been arranged that another friendly guard named Conrad would mount Watchtower Seven and give an all-clear signal to the Camerons with his cigarette lighter. In their locked hut, the men were stuffing rags under their bed sheets to make them look occupied, drawing straws to decide who was to go out first, and taking up positions at the window.

The hours passed, and still there was no signal. Perhaps it was all a trap, or maybe the guard had been found out. Sevilla was also waiting and waiting for Conrad to climb the watchtower, but the man had gotten cold feet. Finally, at three in the morning, Sevilla himself slipped away from his drunken chief and scrambled up into the watchtower. With shaky hands, he lit his pipe. The signal.

Relieved beyond measure, Bégué inserted the key in the lock, turned it, and opened the door. It creaked painfully despite having been oiled the previous day. One by one the men ran to the fence where the barbed wire was held slightly apart by trestle tables built by Bégué (for their redecoration of their hut) from old planks of wood. A piece of old carpet was thrown down to stop their stomachs from being torn to shreds as they crawled through. They wriggled through the barbed wire as quickly as they could while the seconds counted down until the next patrol came round.

A couple of miles away, a curly-haired getaway driver named Albert Rigoulet was waiting for the escapees in an old Citroën truck parked in a leafy hollow. The men sprinted through the darkened woods in twos and threes and jumped in the truck. When they had all made it, Rigoulet sped them away into the night.

At daybreak, one of the remaining prisoners started shouting about the disappearances, swearing (just as he had been instructed) that he had noticed nothing unusual. He had also relocked the door and discarded the key. The alarm was sounded immediately, and vast numbers of Vichy police swarmed into the surrounding area. As expected, Gaby was promptly arrested, but Virginia had advised her to create a cast-iron alibi well in advance, and she was released soon after.

Both the Nazis and the Vichy government knew full well that the Allies had pulled off a spectacular escape and a major publicity coup. Virginia wanted the police to believe that the men were already back in England, so she had Germaine's prostitutes, doctors, and hairdressers deliberately start rumors that a dozen men had been picked up in a field by an RAF bomber. In fact, Rigoulet had driven the Camerons a mere twenty miles before dropping them off. They lay down in the springy heather for an hour while he disposed of the truck. Then he reappeared and led them on foot across hills densely shaded by walnut and sweet chestnut trees, far out of the reach of any vehicles.

Jean Pierre-Bloch recalled arriving at "a dilapidated, abandoned house and barn" around noon, and being thrilled to discover that "with admirable organization someone had prepared for our visit." The cupboards were stocked with biscuits, jam, razors, and even soap—a nice Virginia-style touch that went down very well.

For two weeks, the Camerons hunkered down, sleeping during the day and taking only a brief silent walk outside at night, straining their ears for any unfamiliar sound and scouring the dark for movement. Finally, the fuss started to die down, and the men made the journey to Lyon. They traveled in small groups, some on the train, others by truck. Everyone made his way, as instructed, to the Grand Nouvel Hôtel, where they knew Virginia would be waiting to prepare them for their journey into Spain and ultimately Britain.

On August 11, Vic Gerson sent a telegram to SOE: "All Clan Cameron repeat Clan Cameron safely transferred to Lyon repeat Lyon. First party leave next week." For the first time in a long while, there was quite a celebration in SOE headquarters on Baker Street.

Although Virginia's work had taken place behind the scenes, it had been crucial to the operation's success. But she was modest about pushing herself forward for praise. Indeed, many of

Clan Cameron, the twelve SOE agents (shown here with other helpers), whom Virginia helped to escape from Mauzac prison camp.

the Camerons themselves were unaware of the full extent of her role. However, her closest lieutenants and, later, her superiors in London, knew just how much she was responsible for. The way Virginia Hall and Gaby Bloch inspired, led, and drove forward to the very end such a "daring rescue operation" right "under the noses of the guards" became an SOE legend. After researching the Mauzac events in detail, official SOE historian M. R. D. Foot had no doubt that Virginia had been the "lynchpin" of the entire operation.

Later, after the liberation of France, SOE finally acknowledged the true extent of Virginia's contribution to a "very great number" of escapes, most of all Clan Cameron from Mauzac. An internal F Section memorandum, written on November 21, 1944, recorded for posterity that "many of our men owe their liberty and even their lives" to Virginia Hall.

CHAPTER 10

HUNTED

The daring breakout of Clan Cameron caused uproar at German headquarters in Berlin, and prompted Hitler to unleash a brutal crackdown on the Resistance in France. Repeated attacks on factories, freight trains, German cars, power lines, and a government recruitment office in Lyon proved to the Nazis that the Vichy administration was incapable of controlling the threat. It was also clear that the Resistance was now a significant menace to the German war machine. To combat it, the French would no longer be allowed any degree of independence in the Free Zone.

The Third Reich decided to lay the groundwork for a full occupation of France. Their first step was ordering the Vichy government to issue five hundred French identity cards to the Gestapo. Under the name Operation Donar, after the Germanic god of thunder, the Nazis planned to infiltrate Resistance networks throughout the Free Zone. Hundreds of double agents—spies who would pretend to be on the Allied side but who were actually loyal to Germany—would root out and eliminate Resistance units in cities across the south.

Lyon was their primary target. Both the Gestapo and the Abwehr harbored suspicions about connections between the US consulate in Lyon, where Virginia was still a frequent visitor, and the Resistance, and kept it under close surveillance. The Abwehr had deduced by now that their principal target was a woman—a woman with a limp called Marie Monin, who they believed to be either English or Canadian. The methodical Bleicher would not move in until he was sure who she was and who she was working with.

Meanwhile, the Gestapo's most ruthless killer was also taking an interest in Virginia. Klaus Barbie, who was known as the Butcher of Lyon, was consumed by an obsessive desire to crush SOE and everyone associated with it. He viewed it as the backbone of the whole Resistance threat. Within a year Barbie would be awarded the Iron Cross (reputedly by Hitler himself) for torturing and murdering thousands of Resistance fighters. He knew they were getting closer to the "Limping Lady of Lyon." Someone would break under torture and denounce her. He would make sure of it.

Virginia was unaware of the dark forces closing in on her, and her health was better and her spirits higher that August than they had been for some time. The Mauzac triumph had cheered her, and at the beginning of the month, Nicolas Bodington came to Lyon for discussions about her future. Virginia made a convincing case for continuing in her post, insisting that her high-placed friends would keep her out of danger.

Bodington relented, and recommended to SOE that it should cancel Virginia's recall. After all, he had been the one to take a gamble on her, and it had certainly paid off. SOE agreed, and asked the *New York Post* to commission more articles from her to maintain her cover.

While he was in Lyon, Bodington sought to calm the rivalries among the SOE agents there and to make clear who was commander in chief. Perhaps he thought it was a good idea to have a Frenchman in charge. Perhaps SOE's F Section was simply reluctant to promote a woman. Whatever the reason, to many Resistance fighters' horror and to Virginia's dismay, the position went to Alain.

It had been almost a year since Virginia went behind enemy lines, and she was the only woman who had been dispatched by F Section in all of that time. At first it had been an advantage to be a woman working undercover. Most Germans, fed propaganda about how women's lives should revolve around *Kinder*, *Kirche*, *Küche* (children, church, kitchen), had assumed that fragile females would hardly get involved in something as dirty and dangerous as the Resistance. Now, as Virginia was fully aware, the Nazis' opinions about women's capabilities had changed dramatically.

The Gestapo discovered that more and more local women were playing an active role in the Resistance. Many took the particularly dangerous job of messenger, transporting money, letters, and weapons between agents. One hid so many firearms in her baby carriage that the whole contraption nearly collapsed under the weight. Couriers also kept a lot of information in their heads, including agents' names and addresses. Therefore, if caught by the Gestapo, women were subjected to the worst forms of torture the depraved Nazi mindset could devise. One particularly vicious method was threatening to harm their families.

Yet Virginia's success opened the gates for other women agents. While they went on to play what Buckmaster called "an extremely important role" in the war, they paid a high price. Thirteen of the thirty-nine women sent into France by SOE—one in three—never came home. That was compared to one in four of the four hundred or so male agents.

Virginia, shown here with her brother, John.

The higher death rate for female spies was due in part to the fact that many were couriers, which involved travel and therefore a greater risk of meeting patrols while carrying incriminating material. Later on, their work as radio operators put them in danger too. Thousands of French female Resistance fighters also paid with their lives. Their typical role of providing safe houses made them vulnerable to betrayal. One in five women who took in people or supplies was executed.

Virginia herself just kept going. She was busier than ever and was working with other Allied intelligence agencies from Poland and Belgium, as well as with the British MI6. SOE commanders warned her that people were taking advantage of "her kind heart," but she could not resist any of the many opportunities for intelligence gathering and network building that came her way. During August alone, she worked with twenty-five SOE-trained organizers and six pianists in the Free Zone, and eight different networks across the whole of France. She helped them with sabotage, parachute drops, and intelligence gathering, and received two thousand pounds of supplies delivered by sea.

SOE decided that it was time to scale up from petty attacks on Nazi and Vichy authorities to "big bangs." For the first time there was also talk of sabotaging industrial sites and identifying military targets to support a future Allied invasion. Virginia's months of preparation appeared to be leading to real action, and she wanted more than anything to see it through.

Parachute drops of arms and explosives were stepped up, and dozens more agents arrived in France. Some carried false-bottomed suitcases concealing explosives, and SOE masterminds had invented a range of ingenious devices: milk bottles that exploded if the cap was removed, loaves of bread that blew up when cut, and fountain pens that squirted poison. Perhaps the most popular was fake horse dung that detonated when driven over. There were also tiny but lethal charges that could be inserted into cigarettes, matchboxes, bicycle pumps, fountain pens, hairbrushes, and—perhaps most usefully—railway engines and fuel tanks.

Virginia was ordered to dispatch Ben Cowburn to sabotage the railway network in central France, aided by the groups of men they had been training. She also received delivery of two hundred thousand francs for teams taking control of Lyon's Perrache railway station and a nearby airfield, as well as blowing up a power station.

Meanwhile, SOE had finally realized that Alain was "a bluffer, vain and boastful," and recalled him to London. His behavior made him a threat to himself and others, and he had not achieved anything significant in his time in France. "We are all vastly relieved . . . that A has departed," Virginia reported. She was, however, in desperate need of the right sort of support, and asked SOE for "a first-class man, experienced, authoritative, willing to take responsibility and lead an unpleasant life" and, most of all, "not complain." She was tired of playing mother to men who behaved like unruly children, like one agent who lost nearly thirty thousand francs and his papers on a train.

She continued to extend her sphere of influence, particularly within Paris—which meant taking a grave risk. France's capital was the target of the most brutal Gestapo raids, and the Resistance there was constantly being decimated by mass arrests.

Unfortunately, Virginia's renown in Paris would cost her—and many others—very dearly.

Virginia knew she was being watched. There were a handful of faces she saw too often to be a coincidence, and the sight of the Gestapo's dreaded black cars was becoming too frequent. The sound of footsteps behind her gave her the shivers, and she had some narrow escapes. She took to the backstreets, melting into Lyon's covered passages, clinging to the shadows, constantly glancing up at the windows above her in case of sudden movement.

Earlier that month, on August 4, a priest in black robes rapped on the double doors of Dr. Rousset's office in Lyon. When he was admitted, he demanded to see Pépin, and explained that he was the new courier for a Resistance network in Paris. He handed over a number of microfilms in an envelope marked "Marie Monin" for dispatch to London.

Rousset had never seen the man before, but he was happy to take the parcel. A Catholic himself, he was reassured by the visitor's religious garb and, of course, the fact that he knew the protocols, such as the code name on the envelope, his own code name of Pépin, and the right passwords.

The priest asked for the two hundred thousand francs that were due for his network's expenses, but was told that because Marie had not known he was coming, she had not left the money at Rousset's office. Would he care to wait? The priest said that he would not, but that he would be back in a week.

In fact, it was three weeks before he made another appearance, on August 25. This time he insisted on meeting Marie in person, saying that he had important news. Rousset was relieved to see him again and happy to fetch Virginia so she could hand the money over herself. He hurried over to her apartment, checked that the flowerpot was on the windowsill, and knocked softly on her door.

Virginia grabbed an envelope stuffed with cash from behind a cupboard, and followed the doctor back to his office at a safe distance. She slipped past the waiting patients into a side room where the priest named Robert Alesch was waiting. Before her she saw a powerfully built man staring at her with piercing blue eyes. He had a tight mouth and a prominent dimpled chin. He appeared slightly ill at ease as he asked if she was Marie Monin.

When Virginia heard his heavy German accent, right in the heart of her network's headquarters, she froze with horror. The priest quickly explained that he was from Alsace, the border region between France and Germany, hence the strong accent. Virginia reminded herself that he had known Pépin's address and both their code names, and that Rousset had heard reports that Alesch had denounced the Third Reich in his sermons. So, despite a gnawing sense of doubt, she and Rousset decided to welcome him into the fold.

Over the following week, however, Virginia suffered a crisis of confidence. One of her best couriers informed her that a Resistance network in Paris had been virtually wiped out by arrests in mid-August, and that the joint network chief, Jacques Legrand, was in the hands of the Gestapo. Alesch had come to see her after that disaster, but he had not even mentioned it.

When Alesch reappeared on September 2, Virginia confronted him with her suspicions. He was quick to explain himself. He, too, had been worried about Legrand, he said, but he had not wanted to alarm Virginia until he knew for certain what had happened.

Virginia was rattled and sought advice. "Can you check on him and give me instructions?" she asked SOE two days later. "I can't believe he's a phony." Yet neither could she entirely banish the thought. SOE agreed to run a background check on Alesch but came up with nothing. To be on the safe side, they encouraged Virginia to have nothing more to do with him. But Virginia decided that she could handle Alesch and that his intelligence was too valuable to just discard him. In any case, Rousset, whose judgment she valued, continued to believe in the priest.

Once Virginia put her faith in Alesch, her vast army of supporters thought it was safe for them to do so too. It was an error that was to have devastating consequences.

CHAPTER 11

INFILTRATION

On October 1, Virginia met Alesch again, and he supplied her with another apparently exceptional haul of films, papers, and maps of German fortifications for transmission to London. He was really turning into a golden informant. With SOE's blessing, she handed him a hundred thousand francs and even a newly arrived radio set.

However, what looked like high-quality intelligence was, in fact, almost useless. Father Robert Alesch had another name: Agent Axel of the Abwehr, code number GV7162. He had already spent a large part of the money he had been given—by Virginia and others—living the high life in Paris, and was about to move into a gilded eight-room apartment, decorated with fine works of art that had been stolen by his Nazi paymasters.

Originally from Luxembourg, Alesch had realized that his best chance of achieving his personal ambition of becoming a wealthy man lay with the Nazis. In 1941, he became a naturalized German citizen, and he approached the Abwehr with an offer to

Robert Alesch

spy for them. First, he allowed his charisma—and habit of condemning the Germans at Mass—to win over his parishioners' confidence. Local youths confided in him about their work for the Resistance—and were arrested soon after he sold their names to the Nazis. When Alesch subsequently thundered about these arrests from the pulpit, he earned himself the further admiration of his unsuspecting flock. So when he heard of Jacques Legrand's Resistance network and approached them, they saw him as someone to trust.

It made sense to send Alesch to Lyon when, for security reasons, Legrand could not travel. The priest could hide the microfilm in his cassock and use the travel pass that came with his job to cross the heavily patrolled border between occupied France and the Free Zone without interference. He was given Dr. Rousset's address, the relevant code names and passwords, and the package for Marie Monin.

Virginia was now at the center of a vicious German game. The Abwehr had waited a long time to track down Marie Monin, and now they finally had her in their sights. They had penetrated her organization to such a degree that they could intercept and break many of her coded messages, and bit by bit they unraveled her networks. By early October, they even knew that she suspected Alesch of being a German agent. When the time was right, when she was no longer so useful, or when it looked like the Gestapo would get there first, they would move in and arrest her.

After all the recent arrests by the Gestapo, Virginia had a dramatic change of heart. Although unaware of the Abwehr penetration, she finally realized that she had no choice but to leave before the Germans took over the Free Zone. "I think my time has come," she reported regretfully. "My address has been given to Vichy, although not my name, but it wouldn't be hard to guess."

She also suspected that she had lost the support of one of her chief protectors, police chief Léon Guth. To her furious disbelief, he had deliberately increased the number of guards watching a group of SOE prisoners, making a planned rescue mission impossible. "I can't make heads or tails of it," a perplexed Virginia had signaled London. It later transpired that the Gestapo, suspicious about all the recent escapes, had threatened Guth's family if he "lost" any more prisoners or if he appeared to be helping SOE agents abscond.

Virginia wanted to leave openly as the *New York Post* correspondent, fearing that an unexplained departure would create problems for those she left behind. On September 21, she asked SOE to arrange her ticket for a flight from Lisbon so that she could apply for the necessary visas and "clear out if necessary."

In the meantime, Germaine Guérin lent Virginia an apartment because "astounding personnages" had been turning up day and night at place Ollier. The new location was more tucked away, on the sixth floor with a broken elevator. It was a hard climb up the stairs with Cuthbert, but the apartment's inaccessibility helped cut down on visitors. The doorkeeper was a loyal member of the Resistance who kept watch for her.

Virginia's departure became increasingly urgent. On Saturday, November 7, the US consulate contacted her to tell her that the invasion of North Africa was imminent, meaning that a full German occupation of the French Free Zone would soon follow. Their predictions were correct. Early the next morning, a hundred thousand Allied troops, under the command of US general Dwight Eisenhower, landed in Vichy-held North Africa at Algiers, Oran, and Casablanca.

In response, Hitler flooded the Free Zone with his troops and tanks. Virginia had mere hours before the Nazis took full control. Soon, her friends and protectors in the Vichy government and police force would be powerless. German terror would be unbridled, and the Resistance would be crushed. How could she stay and hope to survive?

Virginia rose early and, ever conscientious, spent the day tying up loose ends. Hurrying through the eerily empty streets of Lyon, she bumped into a former French secret service agent who had been helpful in the past. He pleaded with her to leave at once. No French police chief, no US diplomat, no cover as a journalist could help her now. The Nazis knew all about her and would show her no mercy.

She made one final visit to her apartment, packed the rest of her money and a bag of clothes, and lugged it as quickly as she could, Cuthbert permitting, to the station. She made the last train south out of Lyon, which left at eleven o'clock, by the skin of her teeth. Virginia told no one—not even Rousset or Germaine—that she was bound for Perpignan, the southernmost city in mainland France, three hundred miles away. It was a long night. The track meandered through the factories, silk warehouses, and oil refineries of southern Lyon to Marseille, where Virginia changed trains. No doubt she had on one of her disguises to get her through the Gestapo security controls.

Virginia's only chance of escape was on foot over one of the cruelest mountain passes in the Pyrenees. The narrow trail was treacherous and often impassable, even in summer. In winter, the snow could reach waist height. But there was no other way out of France. After a sleepless night, she arrived in Perpignan, twenty miles from the Spanish border near the eastern edge of the Pyrenees. It was a town she knew well, having helped so many others to escape from there. She checked into a hotel and stayed out of sight until the afternoon, when she knew that a contact, Gilbert, spent an hour on the town square every day between 2:00 and 3:00 p.m.

Gilbert immediately spotted the tall American woman he knew as "Germaine" hovering half out of sight behind the trees.

He had done business with her before and signaled her to follow him down a side street where they could talk. A biting north wind cut through the alley, and the November air smelled of snow.

Gilbert agreed to try to find a mountain guide, a *passeur*, willing to take a woman over the mountain, but warned it would be difficult. He didn't know about Cuthbert, and Virginia needed to make sure that neither he nor the *passeur* found out. They would certainly not risk their lives taking someone they thought might slow them down or give up halfway.

The price would be high—nearly twenty times the usual rate—and there would be two others, men Virginia didn't know but who had been waiting for some time. They did not have the money yet, Gilbert said, so she would have to be patient. There could be no delay, Virginia insisted. She would pay for all three of them.

At 7:00 a.m. the next morning, the Nazi military stormed into the Free Zone. They met no serious opposition. Much of the Lyon Resistance, which Alain had led SOE to believe was a mammoth fighting force, did practically nothing. An official report later found that most were "seized by panic" and threw their weapons in the river, noting that "at the first sight of danger their bluff had been called." It would be only a matter of hours before the troops and the tanks occupying towns and cities across the Free Zone arrived in Perpignan, and Virginia would be deprived of her last chance of freedom.

In Lyon's Gestapo headquarters, Klaus Barbie was seething. He ordered thousands of posters to be printed and posted across France. Under a lifelike drawing of Virginia was splashed, in enormous letters, THE ENEMY'S MOST DANGEROUS SPY: WE MUST FIND AND DESTROY HER! A large reward was offered for information leading to the arrest of "Marie Monin." Her luck was surely running out.

CHAPTER 12

ESCAPE TO SPAIN

After nightfall, a *passeur* finally came for Virginia, and with huge relief she slipped into the front of his van. She handed him half the money with the promise that the balance would be paid on the other side of the Spanish border. In the back of the van she could just make out two men huddled on the floor. They introduced themselves as Leon Guttman and Jean Alibert, and thanked her for paying their way. Virginia, ever on the lookout for good recruits, wondered whether she could use them on a future mission. Even now, she was determined that there would be one.

The van took a series of hairpin bends before slowing to tackle the steeply climbing track. It stopped outside a barn in the foothills, and the three fugitives were told to rest. They set off on foot at first light. The morning mist hung like gauze over the path carved through the mountainside by the turbulent Rotja river.

At first the climb was gradual, but after several hours, the terrain grew increasingly steep. Virginia carried her heavy bag on her right side to disguise her limp. As the snow grew heavier and more slippery, the pain in her stump began to wear her down, but she could not fall behind: there was much harder terrain to come, and fifty miles to go.

On they climbed, past hot springs on a grueling ascent to the tiny hamlet of Py. Each step jarred as Virginia dragged her prosthetic leg up the slope, the weight of her bag tearing at her shoulder. On one side of her yawned a precipice several hundred feet deep, and on the other side was a steep slab of mountain with virtually nothing to hold on to or to shelter her from the fierce gale.

The snow was three yards deep in places, but Virginia had no snowshoes nor even a walking stick. Hammered by the sharp wind, her lungs strained for oxygen in the thin air, her head pounded, and she felt dizzy. Her stump was an open, oozing, and bleeding sore. However, she had no choice but to keep up with the men. If she lagged behind, the *passeur* might well take out his gun and shoot her. Step by step she pushed on, up and up. Once again, she drew on her father's words in her vision, about her duty to survive. Nothing in all the hardships of the war came close to the agony and fear of those long hours of endurance.

When they reached the Mantet Pass, at six thousand feet, the guide allowed them to rest in a shepherd's hut and eat some of the sparse provisions they had brought with them (probably just sugar cubes and biscuits). They huddled together to keep warm—Virginia took care to hide her prosthetic leg and her blood-drenched sock. Cuthbert was crumbling beneath her, its rivets slowly working loose under the strain.

It was likely from here that she sent a now-legendary message to SOE—perhaps with one of the new, lighter radios hidden in her bag, or maybe a set that had been stowed away in the hut. It read, "Cuthbert is being tiresome, but I can cope."

The duty officer who took her message in the receiving station, at a large country house in England, had no idea to whom she was referring. "If Cuthbert is tiresome," he signaled back, "have him eliminated."

The next morning, they climbed in single file to eight thousand feet, reaching the top of the pass at midday. From here they looked in wonder at Spain unfolding below them. The *passeur* took the rest of Virginia's money and turned back.

There was no time to rest, however, as they still had another twenty miles to go. They trudged down the long, winding path, limbs now heavy as lead. There were stories about wolves and bears picking off escapees along this stretch, and Virginia urged her companions to push on through the pain, although finding the energy to talk was a struggle. She took care to walk in a way she thought might hold Cuthbert together until the end, but going downhill was even more treacherous. The lack of flexibility in her prosthetic leg meant she had to lean forward, and she feared falling into the void.

Somehow the trio persevered, and they reached San Juan, in

Spain, before dawn, in time for the 5:45 a.m. train to Barcelona, where help was awaiting them. A Spanish police patrol found them on the station platform in a state of virtual physical collapse. The two men stuttered out some excuses, but Virginia explained in Spanish that she was American and had merely been enjoying the mountains. The suspicious policemen took one look at their filthy clothes and arrested them as "undocumented and destitute refugees" before pushing them into the patrol car. They were brought to the police station and then on to the prison in Figueres.

Virginia had helped countless others to their freedom. She herself had escaped France, the Gestapo, and the Abwehr. She had battled through snow and wind over an eight-thousand-foot pass. She had been within an hour of catching a train to safety, a warm bath, and a hot meal. And now she was behind bars.

JUST BEFORE DAWN on the same day, Dr. Rousset was arrested in Lyon on charges of spying and terrorism, and hauled off in handcuffs. Over the following days and weeks, he was subjected to barbaric torture. The Gestapo already knew Virginia's code name and the identities and addresses of many of her associates. They just did not know her real name or where she was. "Where is the 'Limping Lady'?" they screamed. "Who is Marie Monin?" Pépin acknowledged that he knew Virginia, but insisted that he was just her doctor and that he had no idea who she really was, or where she had gone.

Anyone connected to SOE and the Resistance was in mortal danger. In one frantic chase through Lyon's covered passageways, a Gestapo officer caught hold of SOE agent Edward Zeff's foot, but Zeff managed to pull free, leaving his shoe behind in the German's grasp. He made a dash for Spain in February 1943, but was betrayed by his *passeur* in exchange for the large bounty on offer for informing on a Jewish person to the Nazis.

After Virginia vanished and Pépin was arrested, Germaine tried to hold the network together. She recognized the mounting dangers, and frequently altered her routine, but neither her precautions nor her connections, wits, or beauty could save her. On the evening of January 8, Gestapo officials, Nazi paramilitaries, and Vichy police hammered at her door, yelling, "Open up or we shoot!"

Germaine was at home, along with two British SOE agents, brothers Alfred and Henry Newton. She began to approach the door, and the brothers realized she was getting ready to sacrifice herself so that they could get away through the back. What her friends admiringly called her "fiery love and shame for France" came first and foremost; she positively embodied the courage she felt many of her countrymen lacked.

The Newtons pleaded with Germaine to escape with them while she could, but her face was set in steely determination. One brother briefly considered knocking her out and carrying her to safety unconscious. But they would have to clear several walls and more than likely shoot their way to freedom. So with the final

Henry and Alfred Newton pre–World War II, when they were entertainers, 1938.

seconds ticking away until the door was battered down, they did as she asked, and escaped.

Alfred's last sight of Germaine was of her stripping down to her underwear and calling out sleepily: "*Allô?* Who's there? What do you want at this time of night?" Proud and dignified, she pulled on a robe and opened the door.

Germaine was transported in a cattle car to the concentration camp for women at Ravensbrück, north of Berlin, where her head was shaved, and she was given the number 39280 and a uniform—a rough blue-and-white-striped cotton dress and wooden shoes. She was assigned to a hut close to the gas chambers.

IN SPAIN, VIRGINIA was taken to a filthy and overcrowded cell. Although weak, she spent her time plotting her escape. After a couple of weeks, her chance came. One of her cellmates was being released, and Virginia asked her to smuggle out a coded letter for the US consulate. Its apparently innocent chatter about her health and her friends concealed secret messages about her whereabouts, and demanded urgent action to get her out. She signed off, "Best to you all. I've got my fingers crossed and, as usual, chin up and tail over the dashboard. V.H."

The American diplomats were quick to act, and Virginia was released a week later after money changed hands. Finally ensconced in the safety of the US consulate in Barcelona, she took a hot bath, slept in a blissfully clean bed, and made sure her mother, who had been starved of news for months, knew she was safe. Then she snapped back into action, sending a telegram to the *New York Post* to send her five hundred dollars (swiftly reimbursed by SOE) plus a visa and emergency passport to travel to England.

She composed a long report for SOE, which included painstaking arrangements for the people and supplies she had left behind in Lyon. She was unaware, of course, of all the arrests. She also pressed SOE to "do everything possible" to secure the release of her Pyrenees companions Guttman and Alibert, stating she wanted to work with them in the future.

SOE was overjoyed to hear from her and sent congratulations on her release. But, to Virginia's dismay, administrative hitches meant that it was more than a month before she made it to Lisbon and a further month's delay until her flight out. When she arrived in England on January 19, 1943, she was picked up in a polished Humber limousine and driven up to London, where Buckmaster, Bodington, and F Section's new key player, Vera Atkins, gave her a rapturous reception.

Their exceptional American had survived longer in the field than any other agent. She had avoided capture for fourteen months, and had impeccably maintained her cover as a journalist.

She had set up vast networks, rescued numerous officers, and provided top-grade intelligence, laying the foundations for the great Resistance battles that were to come. She had even crossed the Pyrenees on foot in the snow with a prosthetic leg.

At last, Virginia had the time to recover physically. She took Cuthbert to a prosthetics specialist to be fixed and have the rivets redone. The pilot William Simpson went with her—he was having a prosthetic hand fitted—and he marveled at what she had achieved. "For the life of me I cannot conceive how it was possible," he exclaimed about her escape over the Pyrenees. Yet she was "a picture of health and abounding good spirits."

Virginia was extensively debriefed, and was able to share her thoughts on good agents and bad, as well as the lack of radio operators and sets. She was also questioned about Robert Alesch. SOE had belatedly pieced together the evidence and realized he might be one of the deadliest double agents of the war.

What dominated Virginia's thoughts, though, was not her good fortune to be free, but the fate of her friends. As reports came in of one arrest after another, she became increasingly tormented. Was she to blame for their downfall by recruiting them in the first place, and then allowing Alesch access to the network? Should she have left them to fend for themselves while she had taken the opportunity to flee? Whatever the risks, she now knew she had to go back to France. She owed it to them all to continue the fight.

CHAPTER 13

BURNED

On May 17, 1943, Virginia traveled to Madrid, Spain, with a new cover as foreign correspondent for the *Chicago Times* newspaper. Her orders were to devote a couple of months to journalism to establish her credentials before starting on her real task: organizing Spanish safe houses and escape routes for French Resistance refugees.

The job was a compromise: it would get her away from the dull office work she had been doing in London, but it would also keep her from the dangers of France. SOE's Spanish chief (known as H/X) was dismissive of Virginia's talents. He assumed that "much of her usefulness" would come from the traditionally feminine work of "being able to give and accept entertainment," such as tea parties.

Far from giving her the freedom to rely on her wits and run her own show, as she had done in France, Virginia's new bosses set out to control her and to restrict what she could do. "You will see . . . that we have done our best to tie [her] up so that she can have no excuse for undertaking any work without your prior knowledge and approval," her immediate superior, DF, crowed to H/X. There was an equally insulting showdown over money, with DF even suggesting that Virginia's pay—little more than an embassy typist's to begin with—"might be reduced."

It was all a cruel disappointment. Although Virginia was not particularly interested in money, the argument reflected how underrated and disrespected she was by some of her commanders. Where she wanted to be, of course, was in France, at the center of the action. But that had been blocked categorically by SOE's bosses. She was *brûlée* (meaning "burned," or that her cover was blown): she could never go back.

As always, Virginia tried to overcome the obstacles by throwing herself into her work. Now that summer had come, there was a steady stream of SOE agents and Resistance fighters escaping over the Pyrenees. She would alert London to the arrival of a new group with a coded message, such as "Florence's dog has had five puppies, repeat five puppies, of which one is a girl," which meant that five had made it over the mountains, one of whom was a woman. She provided them all with safe houses and papers to help them get back to Britain.

She was particularly happy to be able to assist her "nephews," Marcel Leccia and Elisée Allard, both of whom had helped her in France. They arrived in Madrid thin and exhausted after eight months in Spanish prisons. Bored and disappointed with her posting, Virginia was delighted to be reunited with them,

Marcel Leccia

particularly Leccia, whose dark sense of humor she enjoyed. She considered him one of her bravest recruits, and arranged for him and Allard to receive formal SOE training in London.

By September, though, after four months, Virginia considered staying in Madrid a waste of time. Meeting the "nephews" had reawakened her thoughts of France, as she told F Section in a letter. "I have had the luck to find two of my very own boys here and send them on to you. They want me to go back [to France] with them because we worked together before and our team work is good . . . I suggest I go back as their radio [operator]."

What was the sense of remaining in Madrid when there was so much to be done in France? Her letter continued, "When I came out here, I thought that I would be able to help F Section people, but I don't and can't . . . I am simply living pleasantly and wasting time. After all," she added, "my neck is my own," and she was "willing to get a crick in it because there is a war on."

Buckmaster was firm in his response: "I know you could learn radio in no time; I know the boys would love to have you in the field; I know all about all the things you could do, and it is only because I honestly believe that the Gestapo would also know it in

Maurice Buckmaster

about a fortnight that I say no." He warned her that it would be impossible to "escape detention for more than a few days," claiming that "what was previously a picnic, comparatively speaking, is now real war."

Buckmaster was only doing his job, and he was right about Virginia being fatally compromised. Yet even he was unaware just how much the Nazis had found out about her. By torturing agents and intercepting SOE messages, they had pieced together a detailed picture of her, her work, and her network of contacts.

Even her old friend SOE agent Peter Churchill confirmed her identity under torture by the Gestapo. After six months in solitary confinement, having been beaten unconscious, starving, unwashed, his glasses gone, and knowing his life was in the balance, he finally broke down. The truth was that he believed Virginia was safely out of France, never to return.

Virginia's bosses in Madrid were not sorry to see her go. Her war record and preference for whirlwind activity were an awkward reminder of their own comparative safety and comfort. She arrived back in London in time for Christmas, and was kept busy at SOE headquarters on Baker Street, debriefing returning agents and preparing those about to leave.

In the new year, Virginia started in SOE's school for radio operators at her own expense, even though she was still barred from returning to France. Students were put through their paces on a variety of different radio sets, including the new Type 3 Mark II, a suitcase model weighing some twenty pounds less than the old ones. Virginia was expected to learn to transmit Morse code at a minimum speed of twenty-five words a minute.

Normally the students were confined to school grounds until they completed the course, but Virginia went up to London every Saturday. No one knew why, where she went, or whom she was seeing. It was most irregular.

It was after one of these mysterious trips that MI5, Britain's domestic intelligence agency, received an inquiry about a reference for the American journalist Miss Virginia Hall from the Office of Strategic Services (OSS), a newly established American spy agency. It had been created by President Roosevelt in June 1942, and had a heavily guarded London office not far from the US embassy. The OSS had endured a difficult start because of hostility from the US military and even White House staff, who were appalled at what they considered a sordid spy service that refused to conduct itself like regular armed forces.

While it was well funded, the fledgling OSS was also seriously lacking in experience in the field, and had yet to establish a single network in France. This was in stark contrast to the more than thirty networks now run by SOE. The OSS director, General

William "Wild Bill" Donovan, realized that what he needed was people who knew how the Nazis operated, and who could dodge everything the Third Reich would throw at them. He needed irregular people who could wage irregular warfare. But where to find them? Then, unexpectedly, one came walking through the door.

Helping the OSS was, of course, Virginia's way around Buckmaster's refusal to send her back to France. She knew the OSS was woefully short of operatives with experience, and that even a one-legged woman stood a chance of breaking in—just as she had done at SOE.

MI5 responded to the OSS's inquiry that it had "no reason" to doubt her reliability. They did not, of course, reveal that Miss Virginia Hall was also SOE Agent 3844, and that she had an unparalleled track record behind enemy lines. But the OSS already knew that. It was precisely why they had asked.

CHAPTER 14

SETTLING SCORES

On the moonless night of March 21, 1944, a small boat landed on a beach in northwestern France. First to disembark was an elderly peasant woman, bundled up in shawls and carrying a heavy suitcase. She maneuvered herself out of the camouflaged dinghy onto the rocks and away from the rising tide.

She was followed out of the boat by a man. He stumbled, twisting his knee, and barely suppressed a loud yelp as the woman helped him to his feet. Even though talking was forbidden, he complained all the way up the narrow path onto the headland and through the gorse bushes to the road. At any moment, the German soldiers on guard in the small concrete fort nearby might turn on their searchlights and start firing.

The man, code-named Aramis, was American Henri Lassot. At sixty-two, he was old enough to be his companion's father, even though she looked older than him. She was actually nearly thirty-eight, but Virginia—or Diane, as she was known in the OSS—had gone to extraordinary lengths to age her appearance. Her hair was dyed a dirty gray and worn in a severe bun that sharpened her features. Movie-studio makeup artists had taught her how to pencil wrinkles around her eyes, and a dentist had ground down her healthy white teeth to look like those of a French peasant woman. She wore baggy woolen blouses and several floor-length skirts with peplums that bulked out her silhouette—and concealed her Colt .32 pistol.

Virginia's clothes had been made, distressed, and rigorously checked by Jewish refugees in a secret workshop in London to ensure they looked authentic—right down to the way the buttons were sewn on. The French favored parallel threading while the British and Americans preferred a crisscross pattern. The wrong technique could have given her away.

She was traveling under her new cover name of Marcelle Montagne. Officially, Aramis was her chief, and she was his assistant and wireless operator. It would have been controversial in America at that time to send a woman on a paramilitary operation—and inconceivable to put one in charge. But taking orders from the inexperienced Aramis was not something Virginia was liable to tolerate for long. Nor was she likely to stick to her restrictive brief of finding safe houses for other agents and wireless operators on the run in central France. She had greater ambitions now that she was back in France. And she had scores to settle.

The first test of her disguise came the next evening when she and Aramis arrived in Paris. The ticket gates at the train station were ringed by Gestapo officers scrutinizing passengers, and Virginia knew that if she were stopped, she would be finished. The suitcase containing her radio (which weighed some thirty pounds) dragged painfully on her left arm, but she had to make it appear light and not arouse suspicion. Fortunately, the Gestapo took no interest in the shuffling old woman visiting from the country.

France had suffered a great deal in the year and a half since Virginia had left, and the mood was changed dramatically. Paris had grown even more tense and downtrodden than on her last visit, and everywhere was under surveillance. Schools had become barracks; cinemas, theaters, and cafés had been taken over exclusively for Germans; and the dance halls and jazz clubs Virginia had loved as a student had all been closed down. After years of anti-Allied propaganda on the radio and on billboards, there was hostility in the air, particularly against Americans.

Aramis complained constantly about his knee, and he went completely against the basics of security by talking about how he had hurt it climbing out of a boat. This irritated Virginia: now was not the time to attract attention.

She had identified an area in central France as being strategically important. It was roughly equidistant from the English Channel and Mediterranean Sea coasts, and the local *maquis* was a small and disorganized band of Resistance fighters, almost entirely without guns or ammunition. It was also familiar territory to her from her first mission. The fact that it was thick with Germans and their informants did not deter her.

With Aramis in tow, she set off by train, alighting two hundred miles southwest of Paris. Her priorities were to recruit and train men into flexible and effective fighting units, and to bring in weapons by air to arm them. It had taken her only a couple of days to move on from her original orders—with the admiring blessing of her superiors at the OSS—to conduct the sort of mission she had always wanted.

Virginia's existing local contacts immediately came into use. One of them drove her with Aramis to meet a farmer named Eugène Lopinat in a hamlet near the steep granite gorges of the Creuse river. Lopinat offered them the use of a one-room hut by the side of the road, and said that Virginia could transmit from his attic, using his intermittent power supply. She felt safer there than in Paris, which was overrun with Gestapo. More important, she felt useful.

Such primitive conditions did not appeal to Aramis. He hurried back to Paris, where he found more comfortable quarters with a family friend. Virginia saw him only once a week when he came to her with updates on his progress in finding safe houses for her to transmit to London. His constant grumbling infuriated her, as did his refusal to listen to her advice on security. His regular visits were unnecessary and could well attract unwanted attention—he could send Virginia information for transmission by other, safer means. "He did not seem to understand using couriers or the advisability of so doing and fiercely resented any suggestions," Virginia complained. She also worried about his talkative habits. Her limited patience had now run out: she would find a way to cut Aramis out and run her own mission in the way she saw fit.

Virginia's mother used to tell her that everything she learned in childhood would come in useful someday, and the long summers she had spent with the farm animals at Box Horn Farm in Maryland helped her now to establish her cover as a milkmaid. "I cooked for the farmer, his old mother, and the hired hand over an open fire as there was no stove in the house," she reported. "I drove his cows to pasture, and in the process found several good fields for parachute drops."

On her daily rounds delivering milk, Virginia began recruiting for the Resistance. Within days, locals, from the mayor's secretary to the village postman, had signed up, and word spread that someone was finally taking charge in the area. Virginia was delighted to find "farmers and farm hands willing and eager to help," and set about transforming "peasant squads" into organized guerrilla units. This was exactly what she had wanted to do for so long.

A week later, a familiar face appeared at her door. Elisée Allard, one of her "nephews," had completed his SOE training in Britain, and had parachuted in just a few miles away. Allard had been infiltrated with her other "nephew," Marcel Leccia, and a third SOE agent Virginia knew and liked, Pierre Geelen.

When Allard heard local gossip about an old lady with a strange accent creating a band of guerrilla fighters, he knew it must be

Virginia. No doubt he gasped when he saw Madame Marcelle and her rotten teeth, but then he knew Virginia would go to almost any length to do her job.

The three men were tasked with blowing up German naval headquarters and a railway yard in preparation for a larger operation: the Allied invasion via the beaches of Normandy on France's northern coast—D-Day. Allard asked Virginia to message London that they had arrived safely and were getting down to work. Even though Virginia now worked for the OSS, it felt as if she had never left SOE.

Virginia stepped up her efforts to gather intelligence. She offered to help Lopinat's mother make more cheese so she could sell it to the occupying Nazi forces. Whenever she came across a small German convoy, she would shuffle up to them to offer her produce, concealing her accent with a feigned old lady's voice. This gave her the opportunity to listen in on their conversations using the German she had learned back in Vienna.

German officers across France had seen the wanted posters for "the enemy's most dangerous spy," but no one seemed to find Madame Marcelle remotely suspicious. They were happy to buy her cheese, and the information she gathered about Nazi military plans was to have a significant impact on the progress of the war.

One day, Virginia was in Lopinat's attic, folding up her radio antenna, when she heard a truck pull up outside. She thought it might be Aramis, but, just in case, she hid the suitcase radio under some crates and bits of old furniture. Then she climbed down the ladder and went to answer the door. To her horror, she saw a group of German soldiers outside. Their commanding officer demanded to know what she was doing alone in the cottage. Switching into character, Virginia replied in a croak that she cooked for the farmer and tended his cows. Not satisfied with her response, the officer ordered three men inside to search the building.

In a state of complete terror, Virginia hoped she had hidden the radio well enough. From inside the house she heard crashing and what sounded like furniture being pulled apart, then the scrape of the ladder against the trapdoor to the loft. She tried to work out how far away she would get before being shot. A better plan would be to stay in character and claim that, as an old woman, she never climbed the ladder and had never been upstairs.

What was certain was that if she were arrested, they would discover Cuthbert and realize her true identity immediately. Her heart thumped as the soldiers continued to turn the cottage upside down. At last, they marched back out. The officer came over to her and peered closely at her face. She could feel his breath on her skin. Would he see through her disguise? Under such intense scrutiny he would surely realize her wrinkles were fake.

Instead, he recognized her as the old cheese lady he had met on the road. He proclaimed her produce to be very good, having helped himself to some more cheese inside the cottage, and chucked a few coins at her feet before they all drove away. Virginia remained still for a few moments, leaning against the door for support. Her mind raced over who or what had brought the "wolves" to her door. Was it her accent? Had she been too brazen?

A few days later, she came across the severed heads of four friendly villagers. The Germans had left them on display in the wildflowers beside the main road as a warning to others of what would happen if they joined the Resistance. Suddenly she felt very alone.

CHAPTER 15

BETRAYED

Virginia could not mention these horrifying incidents to her contacts at the OSS in London for fear of identifying herself and her location if they were intercepted. Instead, on April 18, she asked for permission to move her base "due to daily cutting electric current and traveling conditions."

Before she left, Allard and Geelen appeared with the "biscuit box"—the nickname for a new radio weighing just fourteen pounds—that Virginia had been asking for. They also brought bad news: Their mission was in trouble. Leccia had found them hideouts, but their wireless operator had been arrested. "The whole place was teeming with Gestapo," an agitated Allard told Virginia. "Everybody was scared stiff," and now no one would work with them. Leccia had gone to Paris "to try to arrange something else."

On May 1 came the disturbing news that Geelen was feared captured. His most recent radio transmission had not contained the proper security checks, and since then there had been silence.

If Geelen cracked under the Gestapo's torture, the Nazis would know that the "Limping Lady" was back in France. Virginia barely stopped to pack before she fled to Paris on the next train.

Clearly, she had made mistakes. She had allowed too many people to know where she lived, and to gossip about the way she spoke. An impeccable command of French was indispensable for an undercover agent's survival. But Virginia still had an American accent, a fact that the OSS seemed to have overlooked in their haste to dispatch her. (It had not mattered on her first mission, when she was operating as an American journalist.)

As ever, Virginia came up with a solution. She gambled on asking Aramis's landlady, Madame Rabut, whom she judged to be discreet and reliable, to be her travel companion and to do the talking in public when required. Despite the obvious risks, Madame Rabut jumped at the chance to serve and became, Virginia reported, a "very devoted and useful friend."

There was no time to waste. Marcel Leccia had told Virginia about his family's Resistance contacts in Cosne, a town 120 miles south of Paris. The *maquis* there suffered from poor leadership and factional infighting—a common and infuriating problem. Volunteers were also starved for supplies. The Allies would need a viable guerrilla force there to mount hit-and-run attacks on German troops heading north, and to sabotage their communication links before, during, and after the planned Allied invasion. When Virginia informed the OSS of her next base of operations, they readily agreed, but reminded her that the area was "very hot" with round after round of arrests, so to "please be careful."

Virginia and Madame Rabut traveled together to the home of Colonel Vessereau, the town's retired police chief. He had been forewarned by Leccia to expect an important visitor, and he was waiting for her. The local Resistance fighters had little more than pitchforks and broom handles to fight with, and were short of food and clothes. Virginia's appearance was cause for rejoicing.

With her transmitter, she had a direct line to London, a place that had an almost mythical status of hope and supplies for many French. At last they could ask for arms, ammunition, money, and more agents to train their recruits—and they could expect that their call would be answered.

Virginia set to work training Vessereau's men, with the colonel "doing his best as my second." Together they decided to form a *maquis* split into four groups of twenty-five, and then to train, organize, and arm them. Small groups were best for moving quickly and avoiding detection. Indeed, Virginia made clear to the men that their motto should be "shoot, burn, destroy," followed immediately after by "leave."

She directed them to begin small-scale sabotage or "leech" missions: Knocking a hole in the bottom of a German vehicle's gas tank and setting fire to the escaping fuel. Throwing a weighted rope over a telephone wire to bring it down. Jamming railway points by hammering in a wooden wedge. These operations were best conducted at night, in rubber-soled shoes (because they were quiet) and with faces darkened by mud. For the real fight ahead, they would need military supplies. Virginia arranged for a parachute drop of twelve containers of explosives, guns, and ammunition, scheduled for the next full moon, on May 15.

MARCEL LECCIA—NOW considered a sabotage ace by his new bosses in London—was struggling to find the supporters he needed to blow up the railway hub. The Gestapo was decimating the Resistance, and people were too afraid to get involved. To his relief, he was introduced to a medical student, code-named Lilias, who offered to help.

Lilias said he would pick up Leccia and Allard from their safe house and drive them to Paris, where they could make useful contacts. Waving goodbye to them was Leccia's fiancée, Odette Wilen (code name: Sophie), also on a mission in France. She and the instinctively more cautious Allard did not quite trust Lilias. Where was he getting his gasoline? But the headstrong Leccia thought he could handle Lilias, and gambled on him being the breakthrough they urgently needed.

Tragically, Lilias was yet another double agent, and he drove Leccia and Allard straight into the hands of the enemy. News of their fate emerged only after Leccia persuaded a prison guard to smuggle out a message. Soon after, they were taken to Gestapo headquarters in Paris.

In floods of tears, Sophie raced down to tell Virginia what had happened. The war had already caused Virginia such heartache, but this news was devastating. The "nephews" had shown such bravery in coming back to France, with her encouragement, and they had paid a terrible price.

And it was not only their lives that were now on the line. At least three imprisoned agents knew Virginia was in France, and two knew she was in Cosne. There could be no doubt that the Gestapo—and Klaus Barbie himself—had now heard that Virginia was back in France. Even though the parachute drop she had organized had yet to take place, she had to leave, and fast.

Only Colonel Vessereau and his wife knew where she had gone. Virginia asked them not to tell anyone, although she kept in constant contact with both of them via another courier. It was frustrating not to be able to command the next stage of the operation.

For her next location, she moved fifteen miles away to an area considered particularly overrun with Germans. At least 10 percent of the locals were believed to be working for the enemy, and many of them were making a lucrative living in the process. Enormous sums of money were offered as a reward for information on the location of the *maquis* camps, which the Germans then attacked with mortars and machine guns. Once again, Virginia seems to have shown a remarkable insight into people and an equally remarkable power over them. Her new landlady, Estelle Bertrand, no doubt understood the risks she ran by taking in Madame Marcelle.

Virginia holding two lambs at Box Horn Farm.

The weather throughout the spring of 1944 was miserable, but Virginia went out in the rain and wind almost every day, sliding in the mud in her wooden clogs and peasant disguise. She tended goats for a local farmer, taking care not to talk to anyone. Some of the fields and roadsides had been mined to guard against Resistance ambushes, but Virginia worked out where to stand, leaning on a shepherd's staff while eavesdropping on German soldiers' conversations. When she opened her radio case at night, she had plenty of intelligence to share. And when the time came, on May 15, for the parachute drop of weapons she had arranged before she was forced to flee, she sneaked back under cover of darkness to receive the goods.

The thought of her "nephews" in the clutches of the Gestapo never left her. As soon as she was settled in her new quarters, she dashed up to Paris, in disguise, to smuggle a message to them and hatch an escape plan. She received their reply with bitter dismay: "We are eight not three." They refused to leave five new comrades behind. In truth it would be virtually impossible to pull off a breakout of this size from one of France's highest-security jails.

However, it was not in Virginia's nature to give up, and she repeatedly put herself in mortal danger by returning to Paris every week to try and work something out. Then, at the beginning of June, Allard was transferred to Fresnes prison, a move that suggested deportation or execution was imminent. Leccia and Geelen would not be far behind.

CHAPTER 16

TO ARMS

Time was running out on all fronts. The Allies were in a state of alert ahead of D-Day, the invasion of France by sea, set to take place on June 6. A week earlier, London had signaled Virginia: "Period of activity is commencing. Stop. Please communicate before next Friday [June 2] all information gathered since your arrival concerning large movements by train or road. Stop."

Since then, she had been transmitting every detail on German convoys, their size, regiment, route, and supply lines—high-quality intelligence that made its way all the way up the Allied chain of command. There was virtually no time for sleep, and every night she tuned in to the BBC French Service on the wireless radio to listen for prearranged coded messages that the invasion was about to take place.

The Nazis had stepped up their brutal repression of the Resistance. Anyone even suspected of links to the *maquis* was likely to be executed on the spot. Virginia heard that there was gossip going around about why the lights were on in Estelle Bertrand's attic late into the night, and she had also noticed German radio-detector vans touring the lanes, obviously having picked up her signals. To protect her brave landlady, she swapped houses, and just before D-Day she installed herself at a different farm.

While Virginia was playing cat and mouse with the Germans in France, her mother was following progress of the war in Europe in the newspapers. Mrs. Hall had heard nothing from her daughter for months, but knew her well enough to suspect that she was in danger somewhere. In April, she had written to a Captain Grell, an American based in London, whose address Virginia had provided before she left for France. More than a month later, on June 2, a Charlotte Norris in New York finally responded to Mrs. Hall's letter on Captain Grell's behalf. She apologized for being imprecise for reasons of security, but added that "your daughter is connected with the First Experimental Detachment of the United States Army" (without revealing that this was a front for the OSS). Virginia was "doing important and time-consuming work" that had "necessitated a transfer from London" and had reduced "correspondence to a minimum." She added, "Please feel free to write to me when you like, Mrs. Hall. We are in constant contact with your daughter and are immediately informed of any change in her status. I shall be happy to communicate whatever news I have of her."

There is some discrepancy in the records about where Virginia was when she heard that D-Day was finally underway. One version is that on the evening of June 5 she was with Estelle Bertrand and a few other supporters listening to the radio at her new home in

Cosne. They were tuned to the BBC's French broadcast, which started as it did every evening: "Ici Londres"—translation: *London here*.

On this particular night, the announcer followed with the coded message "Blessent mon coeur d'une langueur monotone" (*Wound my heart with a monotone languor*). These words, from a poem by Paul Verlaine, signaled the news Virginia had been waiting for since her first days as an agent, three years before: the return of Allied armies to French soil. All she had been through—the pain, the grief, the fear—was in preparation for this moment.

Huge convoys of ships were moving through the night to their battle stations in the English Channel, and the first wave of 150,000 men under General Eisenhower's command was preparing to land on the long sandy beaches of France's northern coast, where they would face the steel and fury of the German army.

There followed no fewer than three hundred coded "action messages" during the broadcast, each one instructing a network to carry out prearranged attacks on railways, bridges, and telephone lines. Now it was up to the Resistance to do its part to make the largest invasion by sea in history a success.

"A wave of elation spread" over France, Maurice Buckmaster of SOE later recalled. "Arms were brought down from lofts and dug up from beneath cellar flagstones. Uniforms were brought out and buttons polished. France was ready to help in her own liberation."

News of the landings galvanized Virginia's entire region. She ordered the groups she had so recently armed and organized

Virginia's network of Resistance fighters blew up a railway bridge in August 1944, sabotaging German supply transports.

to swing into action: paralyzing enemy communications by cutting telephone wires, packing explosives on roads and railways, blowing up bridges, and even removing signposts to confuse the Germans who were rushing north to Normandy to help repel the invaders. Others laid SOE's explosive horse dung on the main roads, taking pleasure in watching German vehicles getting flung into the air. Convoys now screeched to a halt every time they saw droppings—genuine or not—causing hours of delays.

Across France, the sabotage efforts of the Resistance were more successful than anyone had dared hope. But all too often, French fighters were let down by lack of supplies. For that reason, every Resistance chief in the region urgently wanted Virginia's help to call in more guns and explosives. She roamed over hundreds of miles of countryside, barely eating or sleeping, inspecting Resistance groups for reliability and transmitting her recommendations back to OSS headquarters. Motor transport and gasoline were rarely available, so, incredibly, she made many of these trips by bicycle.

One Resistance chief, "Colonel Colomb" (real name: Count Arnaud de Vogüé), lacked sufficient arms to attack the convoys passing through his area. His only hope was Diane, the legendary "English" radio operator, who spoke atrocious French but who seemed to have the ear of London. Due to her rigid security measures, he had failed to find a way to contact her.

Finally, he asked his friend Philippe de Vomécourt (the unreliable SOE agent who had once been known as "Gauthier" and was now "Antoine") whether he knew how to contact her. Antoine immediately guessed Diane's true identity and found a way of sending Virginia a note. The answer came straight back, confirming it was her by the use of her old Lyon field name. "I salute you also," she replied, "from Marie to Gauthier."

Virginia agreed to a rendezvous with Antoine and Colomb deep in a local wood. In Lyon, Antoine had gone out of his way to make her life difficult, so she wanted to project all the authority she could muster. She shed her old peasant woman disguise for the occasion, so that she looked and sounded like the toughened guerrilla leader she had become. As she approached through the trees, Antoine saw that she was "the same extraordinary woman who I had known, hiding brilliantly her artificial leg with big strides." He now appreciated that "Virginia Hall was not to be measured by normal standards."

Virginia was cautious, and would not agree to help Colomb until she satisfied herself as to his integrity. She questioned him in detail and inspected his men before deciding his "group was good" and signaling London to send him supplies.

Just five days later, Sten guns, ammunition, explosives, and detonators poured from the skies and were expertly distributed by Virginia. Shortly after the first drop came a second one, bringing a dedicated radio operator for Colomb's group. Virginia was now a power in the land; it was she who decided whether Resistance groups would be backed by the Allies or left to wither without support.

With her constant traveling to inspect groups of guerrilla fighters, she had not had time to work on the Paris escape plan. Not long after her meeting with Antoine and Colomb, she heard that Geelen and Leccia had also been sent to Fresnes prison for deportation to Germany. Her best hope now was that with US troops advancing toward Paris, she would be able to spring the "nephews" and their friends in the ensuing chaos or, failing that, that they would be liberated by the Allies.

For now, though, Virginia was overstretched. She was transmitting for several different groups in a crucially important part of France, and providing what would later be ranked as vital intelligence on troop movements. She was also involved in training, directing attacks and sabotage, and ordering and receiving parachute drops. With success, however, came an appalling price. In response to one of her group's ambushes, the Gestapo looted and torched three villages. In one, they massacred twenty-seven residents, including a priest.

Virginia had brought in fifteen parachute drops supplying arms, ammunition, wireless operators, organizers, food, medicines, and much else besides. She had gathered and armed eight hundred fighters to form the nucleus of what rapidly became "significant" forces of around twelve thousand men "ready for combat." Yet she had still not been given command of her own band of guerrillas. That was about to change.

She sent a message to the still-struggling Aramis in Paris to tell him she was "leaving for parts unknown following orders." And then she vanished.

CHAPTER 17

THE VILLAGE ON THE HIGH PLATEAU

On June 14, Virginia made the two-hundred-mile journey to Le Chambon-sur-Lignon, a village about sixty-five miles southwest of Lyon. She had received orders to inspect the local *maquis* there, described in a radio message as "a trustworthy group of disciplined men, ready to take military orders," and was told to report back on its quality, size, and needs.

Virginia was accompanied by Madame Boitier, her new landlady and chaperone. As they approached the village on the high plateau, the terra-cotta roofs and pots of geraniums typical of southern France gave way to slightly forbidding-looking houses of gray basalt and granite, whose tiny windows were designed to keep out the wind and cold. The sturdy stone roofs were capable of bearing the heavy winter snow, which would cut off the plateau for weeks at a time. The place felt like a land apart, a mysterious plain suspended in the skies, whose people were sometimes likened to the Amish in America. It was unlike anywhere else in France.

Closed off geographically, Le Chambon had a proud tradition of sheltering the persecuted, and was a magnet for those fleeing from the Nazis. As Virginia was to discover, virtually every family in the area was hiding at least one person on the run.

On arrival, the two women walked up to a hamlet above the village, where Virginia knocked on the door of a children's home. A tall, thin man with an earnest face answered. Virginia, dressed as her own age in a plain summer frock, asked if he was Monsieur Bohny and said she was a Belgian journalist reporting on conditions for children in France. She began to ask questions about his work with orphans and malnourished children.

Although somewhat mystified by this woman with her anglophone accent, Bohny invited her inside. He was wary of giving anything away, knowing all too well the threat to his young charges, many of whom were Jewish and in hiding from the Nazis. After about an hour getting nowhere, Virginia confessed that she was "English" and that, in reality, she was not interested in the children so much as looking for a way to contact the *maquis*.

Like many on the plateau, Bohny was a pacifist and had taken a vow to oppose violence. He refused as a matter of principle to assist any form of armed struggle, and said that he could not help her. Clearly, whoever advised Virginia to approach Bohny had made an error. She now thought her entire journey had been in vain. Dejected, she and Madame Boitier checked into a local hotel for the night.

But that same evening, Bohny mentioned the women's visit to

a tutor at the home. The tutor happened to be in the local *maquis*. He in turn told his superior officer in the *maquis*, Maurice Lebrat, about the visit, and Lebrat decided that it was important enough to wake up Pierre Fayol, one of the local Resistance chiefs. Shortly before midnight, Fayol was drifting off to sleep, submachine gun and grenade by his pillow, when his comrades burst in with the news.

The surprise visit to the children's home had come at a crucial time. Since the beginning of the month, the Resistance had been battling thousands of German soldiers, killing hundreds and delaying the others' journey to Normandy, but they had suffered a bloody counterattack by superior German forces who then destroyed local villages in revenge. Just three days before, Resistance fighters had been forced to retreat into the mountains after losing hundreds of men. They feared worse was to come. The German air force had already machine-gunned a village on the edge of the plateau.

Yet there had been virtually no Allied supplies of weapons or ammunition. A week after Allied forces had landed on the beaches at D-Day five hundred miles to the north, the two hundred or so men at Fayol's disposal were ready and willing to fight, but had almost nothing left with which to do so.

"We didn't have the time to check out who she was. We needed to see her straight away," Fayol concluded. "It was just possible she might be able to help us."

Ignoring the curfew, Fayol and his men went to Virginia's hotel room and quietly knocked. In all his life, Fayol had never come across a woman like the tall, battle-hardened figure who answered the door in the heart of the night.

Pierre Fayol

Virginia got straight down to business, firing one question after another: What is your rank? Where do you operate? Who gives you orders? Have you set up parachute drop zones? Can you summon forty good men? What do you need? And lastly, with considerable force: Will you execute my orders without question? Upon hearing Fayol's replies, she instructed him to come back with a car at eight so that they could go look at the drop zones.

A car was requisitioned—no easy feat in wartime—and Fayol pulled up at the hotel with two other *maquisards* at the appointed hour. They toured nine possible drop zones. Virginia had a system for each one: First, she paced out the dimensions. The area had to measure about half a mile across on flat, dry ground with no obstacles or dips. She tested the strength of the wind by holding up a handkerchief: if it failed to fly fully horizontally, then the wind was less than fifteen miles an hour and would be good for parachuting. She noted the coordinates, then chose a code name (always a fish) and a recognition letter to be transmitted by lamp in Morse code to the pilot of the approaching plane. Each zone also had a specific message attached to it.

Her favorite drop zone was on the highest part of the plateau. She gave it the code name Bream, which had the recognition letter *R*, and a few hours ahead of a drop, the BBC French Service would announce, "Cette obscure clarté qui tombe des étoiles" ("This dark light falling from the stars," a line from the play *Le Cid* by Pierre Corneille), which would allow a reception committee of about thirty men time to prepare and secure enough vehicles to transport the goods quickly.

Virginia was impressed by the possibilities for successful parachute drops, and said that she would send a positive report to the OSS in London, who would make the final decision. Sitting above them on a large rock, she told the men that they were competing with other deserving groups for limited resources; indeed, some groups had been waiting five months for a drop. "Money, though, I can give you today. It is right here," she said, patting her belly.

Later that afternoon, they gathered in a smoke-filled room behind a sewing supply shop. Virginia opened the money belt around her waist and handed Maurice Lebrat a wad of thousand-franc notes. "Here's 150,000 francs. Count them."

Lebrat thumbed through the money. "There's 152,000 francs."

"Count again. There's definitely 150,000."

He did as he was told, but insisted she had given him 2,000 francs extra.

"Ah!" Virginia smiled. Lebrat had passed her integrity test.

She gave the men a scrap of paper with a name, an address in Cosne, and the password "I have come on behalf of Jean-Jacques." They could, if needed, leave a message for her there. Then she left and returned to her frantic rounds assisting other Resistance groups in central France.

On June 17, Virginia signaled to London that Fayol's group in Le Chambon had at least two hundred "excellent and well-led" men, capable of increasing rapidly to five hundred. She recommended that two OSS officers be sent in to take charge, along with a radio operator and an adequate supply of arms.

Her OSS commander thanked her for her excellent work, and suggested that she herself should be the radio operator for the mission. Also, she was officially to be given command for the first time. Before relocating, Virginia wanted to see through a series of parachute drops in Cosne, and also to settle in the new radio operators who would replace her there.

Fayol grew impatient when there was no word from Virginia after two weeks. The money had been useful, but by early July—a whole month after D-Day—his men still had no guns or explosives. The proximity of the fighting was provoking panic, particularly after a nearby battle saw the deaths of hundreds of locals and fighters. The Germans were moving en masse toward Normandy from the southwest of France, shooting and burning everyone and everything in their path. Without arms, Fayol's men could not join the fight against them.

Finally, he could stand it no longer. Fayol dispatched two emissaries to find Virginia and bring her back: Jacqueline Decourdemanche, a teacher whose husband had been shot by the Germans, and Eric Barbezat, a local bookseller. They cycled for forty miles and then took a night train, arriving in Cosne on the morning of July 6.

Jacqueline went alone to the address Virginia had given Fayol and miraculously found her there—she never stayed anywhere for more than a few hours. Virginia had been about to leave for the train and grabbed the three suitcases waiting in the hall. One contained her clothes, one her radio set, and one an assortment of firearms. Jacqueline marveled at Virginia's serenity, knowing they would have to pass through several security checkpoints on their way. If caught, Virginia faced certain death. Yet, despite the dangers, she looked radiant, like she had found peace in the middle of deadly turmoil. She exuded a "remarkable calm" despite the "contents of the cases she was carrying."

At the station, they were joined by Barbezat. Suddenly, a railway worker, who assumed correctly that Virginia was foreign, whispered a warning to them that the Germans were expected any minute. He beckoned for them to hide in a shed. They had little choice but to follow him, not knowing for several nerve-racking minutes whether it was a trap. The Gestapo did turn up—they could hear heavy boots on the platform and shouting in German—but mercifully they did not search the shed, and left before the train arrived.

The three clambered on board the train and stood together in the packed corridor. Along the way, as the last rays of the sun were vanishing over the hills, they heard the wail of an air raid siren, and the train came to a screeching halt, sending cases flying and passengers tumbling on top of each other. The doors to the train were flung open, and panicked men, women, and children pushed out, desperate to get as far away from the train as possible before the bombing began.

The planes were almost directly above them by the time Barbezat and Jacqueline reached an exit, but Virginia grabbed their arms tightly before they could jump out. Speaking softly and calmly, she advised them to remain in the carriage. "It's the English who are bombing," she explained. "They know I'm on this train. We won't be touched."

Bombs were raining down all around them now, rattling the train cars and filling the air with acrid smoke. Barbezat looked in astonishment at the completely unruffled Virginia. "But what if the railway bridge at Nevers is bombed?" he gasped.

"Oh, it will be," Virginia confirmed. "But not until tomorrow, after our train has passed through."

She was right. Her communications with the OSS in London meant that she was fully briefed on RAF operations in the region, and also that she could warn them where she was going to be, so she was not put in danger by her own side.

They arrived at their destination early in the morning only to discover that the car that should have been waiting to take them to Le Chambon had not turned up. They stood in vain at the station, knowing they were painfully easy to spot on the wide-open concourse. Finally, as Virginia refused to part from her cases, Barbezat left the two women and went to track down the missing driver at his home.

On his way, a man Barbezat had never seen before made a point of bumping into him and asked for a light for his cigarette. As Barbezat struck a match, the stranger leaned in and whispered not to proceed to the house; the driver had been betrayed and his home put under surveillance. The man then disappeared down a side street. Barbezat never found out how he had known to warn him.

It was clear that Virginia would have to make her own way up to the plateau. They took a bus to a quieter town on the way to Le Chambon, where they checked into a hotel just in time for Virginia to make her scheduled transmission to London.

It would have been foolish for her to stay there for more than a night, because in a small town, her radio signals were easy to track down. Also, her foreign accent, reddish hair, and pale skin made her too obviously a stranger and an object of suspicion for the Germans or meddling locals.

During the night, there was an apparent medical emergency at the hotel. Two paramedics dashed out of an ambulance and up the stairs, returning a few minutes later carrying a figure wrapped head to toe in blankets on a stretcher. The ambulance began to drive slowly toward the local hospital, but soon veered off course and picked up speed. Inside, Virginia emerged from her wrappings. She was back on track, thanks to one of Barbezat's old friends doing him a favor.

The ambulance dropped her on the outskirts of Le Chambon. "Nothing had been arranged about a place for me to live and work," she later complained. She blamed Fayol, for whom she was risking her life. "It was," she decided, "a bad beginning." With nowhere else to go, Virginia insisted she stay with Fayol and his wife in their farmhouse, at least temporarily, so she could begin transmitting.

Marianne Fayol was mesmerized by Virginia's charisma and "very British" appearance, which was ironic given that she was not British at all, but she was careful not to reveal her true identity, even now. Marianne was used to endless requests from the men in the Resistance for more food, more clothes, more medicine, and more cigarettes, and was astonished at how Virginia "demanded no personal comforts and slept for days on strawstacks without complaining."

Even though they shared a house, Marianne had no idea about Cuthbert until she suggested bathing together in the stream by the house, which was the only running water available. Virginia agreed to the suggestion but then added, "If I don't frighten you." She pulled up her skirt to show Marianne her prosthetic leg, clearly nervous about her reaction. It was a rare and fleeting glimpse of her insecurity. In the end, they did not bathe.

Virginia spent hours every day sending and receiving radio

messages, and coding and decoding them at the kitchen table. She had a square of silk the size of a handkerchief printed with fifty columns and fifty rows of random numbers and letters. Each time she used a column for coding or decoding a transmission, she ripped it off the square and burned it.

The Germans now had such sophisticated radio-detection equipment that the job of transmitting was more dangerous than ever. Virginia had to change her base frequently because of low-flying German detector planes, which were more effective in open countryside than vans because of the distances they could cover in the same time. Called "storks" because their wheels hung down on long struts like storks' legs, these small aircraft regularly patrolled the skies for evidence of clandestine radio transmissions. If a plane detected a signal, it was soon followed by bombers that would "paste the place." Even a three-second acknowledgment message could be traced to within half a mile, and a longer message could be pinpointed to within several yards. In truth, Monsieur and Madame Fayol were keen for Virginia to move on, and so was she.

CHAPTER 18

THE MADONNA OF THE MOUNTAINS

A couple of days later, Virginia moved to a barn nearer to the *maquis* camps and the best drop zone. Again she made do without running water and slept on a wooden pallet. It was here that she was finally able to train her own group of Resistance fighters with the help of "Bob," a wisecracking former sailor named Raoul Le Boulicaut, whom Virginia immediately found more obliging than Fayol.

Bob and his men had lived in the mountains for over a year, surviving the harshest of winters on handouts from locals. A third of the group was Jewish, and all of them were young. Bob, who was twenty-four, had managed to maintain discipline, rigidly excluding those he considered trigger-happy or unruly. The men recognized Virginia's devotion to duty and her willingness to endure hardship, so their admiration was mutual.

Until now, they had been making do with a handful of weapons smuggled in overland, but Bob told his men that this

Raoul Le Boulicaut, whom Virginia knew as "Bob."

mysterious newcomer was a "very important figure in the inter-Allied secret services" who would "arrange extraordinary supplies of arms and sabotage materials." Word of such an apparently powerful figure soon spread and brought in more recruits. One of them was a local farmer, Victor Ruelle, who volunteered with 150 of his friends and relations. Virginia was delighted to welcome them in, and set about training them and identifying suitable targets.

Although everyone in the Resistance was united in the cause of defeating the Nazis and liberating France, it was essentially a collection of varied groups that included many different political opinions and strong personalities. There was a particular divide between supporters of the exiled French general Charles de Gaulle and Communists. Virginia was willing to work with anyone who could help her defeat the Germans, and she made sure never to discuss politics, but both sides disliked the fact that she was also working with their rivals, and some were positively obstructive, despite her offers of help.

Indeed, Pierre Fayol began to undermine the very woman who was trying to help him by stoking up distrust of her. How dare a woman, especially a foreign one, be so bossy? Did anyone seriously believe that she could produce the guns and explosives she was promising? Virginia knew very well what was going on, and she also knew that if she didn't conjure up a parachute drop of supplies, her life could well become impossible.

Her next home was a farmstead on a hill above Le Chambon that belonged to Léa Lebrat, a cousin of Maurice Lebrat. Léa not only made Virginia welcome—and fed her extremely well—but also turned out to be yet another pillar of the Resistance. She put her foot down on only one thing: she would not hide guns in the house.

In the absence of electricity, Virginia modified a car battery to power her radio, which Léa's son Edmond charged by pedaling hard on an adapted bicycle. Virginia would sit next to him with her headphones on, tapping out Morse code to the receiving stations in England.

Léa was also sheltering a teacher who was on the run from forced deportation to a Nazi slave labor camp. Dédé Zurbach became Virginia's right-hand man—her driver, assistant, courier, and bodyguard. "She was very active," Dédé recalled fondly, and "demanded our presence at all times."

Virginia bought bicycles for herself, Dédé, Edmond, and Bob, and soon they were pedaling furiously up and down mountains, checking drop zones, and training her team for the vital first delivery. Every evening she listened to the BBC, but while there were plenty of messages for other parts of France, none of them was intended for her. Until she received one, she had no way of proving herself to Fayol.

A painting showing Virginia transmitting messages on her radio via Morse code in July 1944, by Jeff Bass.

It was a nerve-racking wait. Finally, one night, the BBC announcer repeated the sentence "Cette obscure clarté qui tombe des étoiles" three times, which meant that three planes were on their way. As planned, a team of about thirty men rushed to the Bream drop zone, high on the plateau. There were no paved roads, and only a handful of houses scattered around the edge of what felt like the top of the world. On the horizon, the volcanic Massif Central mountains stood out against the fast-fading light.

As the sky darkened to an inky purple, Virginia herself

appeared. There was a collective gasp from the thirty or so men present. The mysterious female English officer they now all referred to as La Madone, *the Madonna*, had discarded her summer dresses in favor of an army jacket and khaki trousers. She wore an orange silk square knotted at her neck (a handy way of hiding her transmitting codes).

The men's chatter came to a halt as Virginia approached. She checked that bundles of sticks had been placed 150 paces apart across the flattest area of grass in a giant Y shape to help the pilots position themselves. Several of the men stood by for the signal to set fire to the sticks. Others took their posts as sentries or readied to start flashing the zone-identity letter *R* in Morse code.

The job of listening for the first suggestion of plane engines belonged to Gabriel Eyraud, an orphan for whom Virginia's *maquis* was a surrogate family. Virginia ordered everyone to be completely silent while Gabriel strained his ears. She had one eye on Fayol, who had arrived to observe. It was clear to all that her credibility—and maybe even her life—was on the line if the skies did not deliver. At last, long after one in the morning, they heard a deep, low sound. As it grew louder, Virginia signaled to the men to light the fires. Soon a throaty roar cut through the darkness, and they could all make out the unmistakable snub-nosed silhouettes of three RAF Halifax bombers.

Trying to stifle their cheers, the men ran to their positions. Down and down the bombers came, to less than six hundred feet above their heads, and when each one reached the center of the

Gabriel Eyraud

Y, the pilots opened their hatches. Showers of silk parachutes carrying huge cylindrical containers thudded onto the ground. The planes rose back up into the darkness, and it is more than likely that the pilots performed a customary dip of their wings in farewell, triggering a wave of emotion inside everyone on the ground. The long, lonely months of waiting were over. This distant part of France was no longer forgotten. La Madone had delivered.

At Virginia's command, the men snapped into action. They split into teams to stamp out the fires, cut the ropes from the twenty metal containers and ten packages now scattered across the plateau, and folded the parachutes into bags. More than three tons of supplies were loaded onto waiting ox-drawn carts and driven to a nearby safe house. Virginia gave them precisely fifteen minutes to finish the job and leave the scene.

Gabriel remembered that "this . . . operation, like those that followed, had to leave no trace. Not to retrieve a cord or piece of parachute fabric . . . or a container could lead to tragic consequences for one person or the group or even the local population as a whole: arrests, torture, death." The containers were thrown into a raging waterfall at the near end of the plateau, and the silk from the parachutes was made into blouses and dresses by the women of the village.

It was a grand haul, and the men felt an exhilarating sense of being brothers-in-arms with strangers many miles away. The longed-for supplies included medicines, battle fatigues with the Croix de Lorraine on the breast pocket, boots (most of the men had only old clogs or even no footwear at all), comforts such as cookies, cigarettes, and packets of Virginia's favorite tea (marked "for Diane"), and, most importantly, weapons.

Virginia's knowledge of the different guns, their qualities and condition, impressed the men, and she expertly divided and repacked them under straw. There was also an S-Phone, a transmitter developed by SOE that would allow Virginia to talk directly to approaching pilots from the ground.

Night after night, more planes brought not only more weapons, but also chocolate, gasoline, bandages, vitamins, more medicine, and, on one occasion, a letter from Virginia's mother. In a sealed container marked "for Diane," there was a package personally packed by Vera Atkins at SOE containing a million francs for Virginia to distribute as she saw fit and several pairs of special socks for Cuthbert.

In total, there were twenty-two drops. The flaming sticks were replaced with battery lamps or headlights; the oxcarts were supplemented with a truck. For Virginia's men, and the villagers who watched in awe from afar, it was as if wherever La

Madone turned up, the night skies came alive with the thrilling roar of Halifaxes.

Inevitably there were errors. The second drop saw an inexperienced pilot release his cargo on another zone, fifteen miles away. When he told Virginia, via the S-Phone, she responded with a furious torrent of curses before dispatching Bob with the truck to retrieve the containers. The planes didn't turn up at all some nights. Others came in too low, and the containers exploded on impact with the ground. Worst of all was when planes were shot down on their way over. One of the BBC's coded messages was intercepted by the Germans, who turned up at the drop zone. Fortunately, that was a night the Halifaxes did not come. The intruders were dealt with, and their bodies were thrown in the Lignon river.

CHAPTER 19

LEADING

The strain of keeping everyone in line took its toll on Virginia. The slightest failure triggered an explosion of temper, swearing, and spitting on the ground in frustration like the scrappy fighter she had become. She was well aware that she was demanding, not least because, very unusually, she was both organizer and radio operator—each a full-time job in itself.

"Diane breathed energy, courage and charm. But she could also be imposing and imperious," said André Roux, one of Bob's men.

"[She] was not always easy to be with," agreed Dédé, "but she left a huge mark on all those who lived by her side. I would not have missed knowing her for all the world."

On the flip side, Virginia treated the youngest *maquisards* like sons. Jean Nallet, a school-age orphan, once told her that he dreamed of becoming a doctor. She made him her medical assistant, giving him the bandages and medicines to look after, and teaching him the first aid skills she had learned as an ambulance driver back in 1940.

Such was her fame and popularity that she was besieged with volunteers. From an initial thirty men, Virginia was now in command of four hundred *maquisards*, whom she organized into five companies. "Unlimited recruitment" was possible, she signaled London, if they could guarantee her the delivery of more arms.

With more supplies, though, came more problems. It was clear in Virginia's mind that the deal with Fayol was that she would finance his group and give them arms, and that in return, they would take orders from her. But he recognized no such obligation, and wanted only to follow orders from the French Forces of the Interior (FFI), the formal name for the French-run elements of the Resistance.

Virginia was far from the only British or American agent to encounter such hostility, but she was determined that the power struggle would not impede the real battle against the Germans, which needed a clear and coherent strategy to succeed. She decided to find another Resistance officer who might help her break the stalemate with Fayol. The FFI expected its fighters to conduct themselves more like a regular army, but it was desperately short of money, so Virginia contacted their treasurer, using a male code name, to offer financing.

Commandant Émile Thérond responded and was no doubt astonished when this masterful woman strode into his hideout offering him money as part of her hard bargain. Immediately Thérond took a more collaborative approach than Fayol, and together he and Virginia struck a deal. If the FFI cooperated with

Allied objectives—including the choice of targets for attack and the techniques to be used—Virginia would hand over a total of three million francs.

The money was enough to fund three battalions of fifteen hundred men, as well as a sustained sabotage campaign, and would put the local FFI on a sound financial footing at last. Thérond praised Virginia's "firm resolution, energy and order and very great organizing ability," and found working with such an "accomplished leader" the "greatest pleasure."

Virginia had gotten her way.

Soon there was a major explosion almost every night, as Virginia unleashed dozens of what she called "bridge and tunnel wrecking" operations to delay Nazi troop movements and cut off their supplies and communications. She sent teams to blow up roads and cut railways, to derail German freight trains, to destroy several bridges, and to ambush convoys.

In London, SOE's Maurice Buckmaster marveled at how adeptly Virginia's groups "violently engaged with the enemy," using the rocky, forested terrain to their full advantage to maximize the element of surprise and then to disappear without a trace. And senior OSS officers acknowledged, "This extremely courageous woman [is] doing fine work."

On August 22, the exhausted but valiant *maquisards* trapped the ragged remnants of a German convoy while Virginia desperately called in more weapons and ammunition. For five days, the fighting raged in the late-summer heat as the enemy tried to push

A *maquisard* on patrol.

its way through. But the FFI held its position under intense fire. The six hundred Germans were running out of willpower, supplies, and hope. Finally, to much jubilation from the French, the Germans surrendered to the FFI.

This moment decisively marked the end of fighting in the region. The area was cleared of the enemy at last. Thanks to Virginia's help, ordinary locals—teachers, farmers, schoolchildren, and factory workers—had financed, organized, armed, and liberated themselves without any professional military support. She sent a telegram to London with the news—and asked for new orders.

The tide of war was turning fast, but Virginia remained in constant danger from the Gestapo, which was now engaged in a frenzy of killing. In Lyon, Klaus Barbie was murdering hundreds of Resistance prisoners at Montluc prison. Virginia had never forgotten her imprisoned "nephews," and had continued to organize food parcels for them. But back in early August, Ben Cowburn had reported the dreaded news that Leccia, Allard, Geelen, and the five others with them had been transported to Germany. They were out of her reach.

Virginia moved once again, this time taking a handsome three-bedroom house halfway between Léa Lebrat's farm and the Bream drop zone. It was well hidden from the road, and she stowed her radio in a disused aqueduct at the back of the property. Somehow she found time to pick mushrooms in the woods and pluck trout from the stream that gurgled past her gate. Léa continued to cook for her, sending her young daughter down the two-mile path through the woods like Little Red Riding Hood with delicious hot meals wrapped in paper.

HIGH ON THE plateau, on the night of September 4, 1944, Virginia was standing by for a US Air Force plane bringing the two American OSS officers she had been waiting for since June. She thought she could hear it in the distance, but when she called the pilot on the S-Phone, he did not answer. Just before dawn she called off the operation.

Lieutenants Henry Riley and Paul Goillot had in fact been dropped twenty miles away. Turbulence had blown them off course, and a brutal landing into trees meant the pair spent several frantic minutes trying to disentangle their parachutes from the branches. Fearing the imminent arrival of the Gestapo, they rushed around in the dark trying to locate the five packages dropped down with them, but gave up after finding only three.

In the chaos of war, no one had told them that the area had already been liberated. They had no idea until they reached Le Chambon and gave the password at the village bicycle shop. Dédé was summoned to look after them, and he explained that Diane could not be disturbed because she was transmitting. He would inform her of their arrival, and she would meet them that evening.

The men had been briefed to act as Diane's organizer and weapons instructor, but they were apprehensive. The OSS had very few women behind the lines, let alone in positions of command. They felt uncomfortable serving beside a woman in combat, to say nothing of taking orders from one, but it had been made clear to them that "in view of her wide experience in the field you will place yourself under her orders."

Virginia was also wary. Would these compatriots of hers help or hinder her?

Henry Riley was an all-American Princeton man: debonair, charming, and highly trained. But it was Paul Goillot, chain-smoking and chatting amiably in "pure slang," who caught Virginia's attention. Eight years younger than her, and six inches shorter, his energy and personality were both larger than life. Born in Paris, he had emigrated to New York as a child after losing his mother, but he still spoke English with a charming French accent.

Paul had worked as a cook, wine steward, handyman, and mechanic. He appeared to be able to fix just about anything and, after excelling on his sabotage course, to blow anything up. Most of all, it turned out he would do exactly what Virginia asked, while also making her laugh. After five long years of war spent alone, Virginia was captivated by him. As it turned out, the two men marveled at what Virginia had achieved and at her desire to do more, despite everything she had endured. They both resolved to help her in any way possible.

At this point in the war, the FFI began to merge with the official French army, and it was made clear that foreign supporters were no longer required. General de Gaulle had seized power as France's provisional president, and had established his government of national unity. Meanwhile, Pétain and the rest of the Vichy government fled to Germany. Millions of French men and women hailed de Gaulle as their political savior, and the Allies, including President Roosevelt, recognized his legitimacy as French leader. De Gaulle rejected any challenge to his authority and told the *maquisards* and other amateur Resistance fighters to go back to their regular jobs and stop pretending to be soldiers.

Virginia yearned to break away from politics and return to where she was happiest: battling the enemy. She had been pestering the OSS headquarters for a new mission, and they finally gave her the go-ahead to help liberate other parts of France. After gathering her most loyal men, she made them an offer. She had food, money, weapons, explosives, vehicles, and a radio. Were they with her?

In the end, nineteen men volunteered—an ideal size for mounting commando-style raids. Most of the men she had hoped would sign up did, including Bob and Dédé. She also had Henry and Paul. Perhaps most important of all to Virginia, she could now, in spite of Cuthbert, join in the fighting herself. She was unafraid to fire a gun, and had shown time and again her courage under pressure. She now had a clear command and proper backup, and could finally emerge from the shadows to fight a more conventional war.

With the green light from Allied command, the Diane Irregulars, as the group became known, were ready to go. They moved off the plateau at sunrise on September 13, dressed in an odd assortment of American military trousers and commandeered Italian leather jackets. It felt good to be on the road, but it was a depressing journey. Locals told them that the retreating Germans were killing randomly and casually as they went. "They shot a man working on a hedge . . . They shot a peasant in a vineyard a hundred yards from the road. They murdered seven woodcutters going home after a morning's work in the forest," reported one eyewitness of the time.

The gruesome sights stiffened the Irregulars' resolve. In truth, they wanted revenge. Virginia went to see a regional Allied commander to ask where they would be most likely to find scattered Germans. He recommended she take her men northeast to Bourg-en-Bresse, up near the Swiss border, to contact an outpost

German soldiers surrendering to the French Resistance, August 22, 1944.

of the US Seventh Army, which was on its way north from the Mediterranean Sea.

When they arrived, Virginia offered her platoon for ambushes in the Vosges, a mountainous area in northeastern France near the German border, where the retreating German army had established a defensive line. Her plan—worked out in impressive detail—was for the Irregulars to attack isolated German units. She later reported that "the reaction to this proposal was immediate and keen and we were told to return in a few days."

CHAPTER 20

THE BOAT ON THE LAKE

While they were waiting for orders, Virginia commandeered a deserted château a few miles away from Allied Command in Bourg-en-Bresse. The pale-stone mansion had enough bedrooms for a small hotel, a grand piano, and even a wine cellar. Henry and Paul "had the boys clean the place up and make it habitable," Virginia reported. "These two officers are extraordinarily efficient at getting things done—just the sort I might have wished for from the beginning."

Later, they gathered on the large balcony overlooking the grounds, which, to their joy, had a lake and even a boat. Despite such relaxed surroundings, the wait to find out about their mission was trying everyone's patience. There was a feeling that the war was rolling away from them and that they were wasting their time. Virginia tried to keep the boys occupied with further military training—a regular schedule of army life consisting of physical workouts, road marches, compass work, and warfare tactics directed by Henry.

It was no doubt with trepidation that Virginia set off a couple of days later, on September 19, to find out whether they were to be deployed in the Vosges as she hoped. She discovered that the regular armies of the Allied powers were advancing faster than expected. The days of the *maquis* were over, and her offer of the Diane Irregulars' help was rejected.

She returned to the château, where she gathered the men and delivered the news that she was obliged to disband the group. Her words were met with an appalled silence. The men wanted to fight the Germans; their quarrel with the enemy could not wait. But Virginia and her fighters had reached the end of the road. She had to bid them all farewell.

Some found it hard to hide their emotions. "I held Diane in great esteem . . . and I deeply regretted that we had to part so abruptly," Dédé recalled. For him, the times in the Resistance with Virginia had taught "tolerance, friendship without calculation and a true notion of service to one's country." It was, he said, "worth being born just for that experience."

To remember their final hours together, they posed for a photograph on the terrace. As commander, and the only woman, Virginia stood at the center of the group, hair pinned up, wearing a tie, khaki pants, and a jacket. Then they lit candles, Paul cooked up the last of the rations, and they raided the wine cellar. After dinner, one of the young Irregulars played the piano, and Virginia joined in with the singing of bawdy songs.

Later that night, Paul and Virginia walked down to the lake,

Virginia (standing) with three officers, including Henry Riley (left) and Paul Goillot (right) at the château she had commandeered.

clambered into the little boat, and rowed across the water under the stars. They had been firm friends since the day they met, and Paul had not challenged or crossed her like so many of the other men she had worked with. His respect for her as a commander was obvious, but now there was something more. At last, Virginia, the battle-hardened secret agent, had found love again.

For years, Virginia had led a life in which trusting anyone could get you killed. That night on the lake with Paul was the first time in as long as she could remember that she felt safe. She wanted more than anything for him to stay with her from now on. If she were to go out on another mission, she informed headquarters soon after, she wanted Paul and Henry "and no one else to go with me."

The three Americans had been summoned to Paris by their OSS commander, but the French men were free either to go home or to sign up with the regular French army. Virginia gave each of them a farewell payment of three thousand francs to get them started on the next phase of their lives. Always meticulous about the money entrusted to her—Dédé once described her as bordering on "stingy"—she asked them each for a signed receipt. She also gave them a letter releasing them from the group. This was so they could prove they had been in the Resistance and no one would accuse them of being French army deserters or, worse, involved with the Vichy government or the Germans. Throughout France, angry people were taking out revenge on Pétain's defeated regime, and thousands were simply shot in the street.

Virginia, Paul, and Henry made their way to Paris, arriving at the joint OSS and SOE Special Forces Headquarters on September 22. Bob, who wanted to reestablish old links with the British, went with them. Paris was a different place from when Virginia had last visited—six months earlier in her peasant woman disguise. The atmosphere was jubilant, with people smiling on the streets and the blue, white, and red French flag draped over balconies and hanging from windows.

Virginia presented herself to Lieutenant Colonel Paul van der Stricht of the OSS, to declare her mission over and to request to be sent back to London. Van der Stricht was pleased that his exceptional agent had returned. The OSS had always had to justify its spending and even its existence to Washington, which considered it a sneaky and underhand spy service. It needed a hero. Now, in Virginia, it had one.

News of her safe return traveled quickly, and a message was relayed to Mrs. Hall: "Virginia continues to be in good health and good spirits, and her work is progressing very well. Reports on the war are full of hope . . . It's not unreasonable to suppose that Virginia will soon be coming home."

But any thoughts of returning to Baltimore were soon shelved. After the triumphant liberation of Paris, the Allies had to face the bitter fact that the war against Hitler and his Nazi regime in other parts of Europe was far from over. Virginia was eager to get back to the fight, and van der Stricht was just as keen to have her. She was summoned back to the field at the end of October 1944.

Virginia and Paul were stationed in the OSS Central European headquarters, a royal palace north of Naples, Italy, where they underwent intensive hand-to-hand combat training. Virginia also worked on perfecting her radio transmissions. Virtually every operator either made their Morse code dashes a little too short or made their dots a tad long—each operator's "fist" or style was as individual as a fingerprint—but she rather resented having to take lessons in something she had been successfully doing under intense pressure in the field.

It was not until March 1945, when the Allied armies were

crossing the Rhine river into Germany and Virginia's patience was wearing thin, that the parameters of her next mission, Operation Fairmont, were finally drawn up. Even then the operation remained uncertain and subject to constant change. Virginia would make her way to Austria—without Paul.

She received a new code name, Camille, and was confirmed as team leader. Her orders were to recruit her own Austrian guerrillas and task them with launching ambushes of German convoys, but her primary mission was to investigate the rumored existence of a Nazi fortress in the mountains. Were the reports true that it was stocked with weapons and two years' worth of provisions for a hundred thousand elite German troops? Once again, Virginia found herself in the eye of the storm, at the sharp edge of the European war.

Incredibly, it was decided that the best way of infiltrating her into Austria was for her to scale a high mountain pass carrying her radio. "Diane, who crossed the Pyrenees on foot at 10,000 feet, seems unafraid of walking," a senior OSS officer observed. Unafraid, yes, but livid that Paul was not allowed to accompany her because of his poor German. They were, she insisted, an inseparable team.

She tried to take control of the infiltration plans herself, even visiting some of her own contacts in Switzerland to find a way for her and Paul to enter Austria together. Her commanders interpreted this as an unwelcome "desire for independence," with one senior officer writing that "Diane's attitude seen from here looks silly . . . [but] I still have hopes to make her see the light."

Virginia resented that her wishes were overruled by superior officers who lacked her experience in the field. Nevertheless, she had to back down, and agreed to cross into Austria without Paul. She was set to cross the border on the night of April 15 when the unexpectedly rapid advance of Allied forces delayed her departure again. Finally, her commanders acknowledged that subjecting her to endless waiting was intolerable. "Something should be done about this woman. If she is a good agent, she deserves better treatment than she has been getting," signaled one clearly embarrassed senior officer.

Events were moving quickly now. On April 30, as the Soviets were shelling Berlin, Adolf Hitler put a pistol to his head and took his own life. Then came the news that the American Seventh Army had met none of the ferocious resistance it had feared from the German people. In fact, in some German towns, the residents applauded Allied soldiers as they marched through. The Nazi mountain fortress turned out to be a fantasy. It had never existed, except in the minds of a handful of die-hard German generals and the imaginations of a few American commanders. In the light of events, the OSS headquarters canceled Virginia's mission.

CHAPTER 21

SURVIVORS

On May 7, 1945, the Third Reich surrendered unconditionally at US General Eisenhower's headquarters in Reims, France. Fighting ceased just before midnight the following day, which was declared Victory in Europe (VE) Day. Even though the war was officially at an end and Virginia's spy work was complete, she felt compelled to return to Lyon—to where it all began. The happiness in her personal life did not cause her to forget the tragedy that had befallen her friends there—or in any of the places in which she had operated across a thousand miles of war-torn countryside.

She was to find out just how heavy a price had been paid. Her visit to Lyon, Paul at her side, was very upsetting. All the fine bridges spanning the rivers had been destroyed by the retreating Germans in September 1944, and the American bombardment in May 1944 had also caused devastation. But far worse than the damage inflicted on the beautiful city was the pain suffered by its people.

Many of Virginia's helpers had been deported to German

concentration camps. Of those, many never came back. The ones who survived the camps and who were liberated by the Allies returned as skeletal figures—sick, weak, and starving. Virginia was deeply saddened by the sight of her former close ally, the wealthy and powerful Germaine Guérin, just back from the Ravensbrück concentration camp, where two-thirds of the inmates had died. Germaine was no longer the joyous force of nature she had once been. Her apartment, closets, and bank accounts were bare, and she was grief-stricken by the news of the death of her friend, Eugène Jeunet.

There are no records of what happened to Germaine's employees, who risked such dangers to extract intelligence from their Vichy and German clients. In the confusion after liberation, many French prostitutes were accused of collaboration and subjected to brutal treatment.

When Dr. Jean Rousset opened the door to Virginia, she was unsure for a moment whether this frail yet dignified figure could really be her Pépin. Rousset had spent eighteen months in Buchenwald concentration camp, and the suffering he experienced there was written all over his face. He never did return to his former jovial self. And Rousset could not cushion the blow of the worst news of all: on the night of September 10, 1944, he witnessed Marcel Leccia, Elisée Allard, and Pierre Geelen being marched out of their hut at Buchenwald and taken to their deaths.

They also discussed the priest, Robert Alesch. It was surely a result of Alesch's treachery that so many of Virginia's helpers had been captured. Rousset agonized about having been fooled by him; he should have known better. But in truth it was Virginia's decision to meet Alesch, to accept his intelligence, and to pay him handsomely—despite her suspicions—that convinced many others he could be trusted. This thought undoubtedly haunted Virginia for the rest of her days.

When Germaine Guérin was arrested in January 1943, her friend Pierre Decley had entrusted Father Alesch with taking her personal treasures into safekeeping. But when Decley returned to Lyon after the city was liberated, he found that Germaine's apartment had been ransacked. Thirteen million francs (some four million dollars today) of cash and valuables had gone missing, and Alesch was nowhere to be found.

Decley alerted the police, who launched an investigation that led them in November 1944 to Alesch's sister, Irma, in Paris. She was living alone in her brother's luxurious apartment. Irma admitted to them that Alesch worked for the Abwehr and that he had returned from Lyon in January 1943 with several suitcases of furs and silverware. The police searched the apartment and found at least some of the items stolen from Germaine's home. The crime was proved—but the suspect had vanished.

In May 1945, Virginia heard that the French police were after Alesch. She had sent OSS headquarters a detailed report on everything she knew about his treachery and the suffering he had caused. This report, along with another one by MI6 (whose agents Alesch had also betrayed), mobilized US Army Intelligence.

Alesch got wind of the fact that the American authorities wanted to question him, and on July 2, he turned himself in to the Americans, expecting that he would be able to make a deal with them and avoid the vengeance of the French justice system. He presented himself as a victim of the Nazis, forced to work for them to save his own skin after they discovered his Resistance activities. Reckoning that the Americans would value a good source on the Abwehr, he hinted that he would provide dozens of names in return for his freedom and financial support.

He also claimed that it was another double agent who had infiltrated Virginia's network and passed on the names of its members to the Gestapo, that he had tried to protect her. Thanks to Virginia's detailed report, the American interrogators were not taken in. They promptly handed Alesch over to the French, and within a week, a long series of court hearings into his treachery began.

WHEN SHE REPORTED on her six-month mission in France, Virginia was generous in her praise of those who deserved it, but in response to the question of who should be recommended for an American honor, she answered with a curt, "In my opinion, no one deserves one." Virginia believed that the respect of their peers, fulfilling their patriotic duty, and restoring the freedom of France should be reward enough. There was, she added, "no reason" for her to be decorated either.

Virginia, undated self-portrait.

Given her views, there was some irony that van der Stricht had set in motion the necessary inquiries for Virginia to receive the Distinguished Service Cross (DSC), the US Army's second-highest military honor, given to soldiers who display extraordinary heroism in combat. She was to be the only civilian woman of the war to receive the DSC.

After the untimely death of President Roosevelt on April 12, 1945, the future of the OSS, the spy service he had established in 1942, looked increasingly uncertain. OSS director Wild Bill Donovan was eager to hold an award ceremony for Virginia to increase his agency's prestige, and he took the unusual step of suggesting it occur at the White House. "Inasmuch as an award of this kind has not been made previously," he wrote to President Harry Truman, "you may wish to make the presentation personally." Truman agreed.

Virginia was embarrassed and alarmed at the thought. Not only did she not care about military honors, but she didn't think it wise for a secret agent to be the focus of a public occasion. She asked her Paris commanders to reject the president's invitation to the Oval Office on her behalf: "Miss Virginia Hall . . . feels very strongly that she should not receive any publicity or any announcement as to her award . . . She states she is still operational and most anxious to get busy. Any publicity would preclude her going on any operation."

Later, Virginia dropped into the OSS office in London to pick up her citation, the official statement about the award. (The medal would be given at a future date in a private ceremony.) A young Women's Army Corps officer remembered the occasion. "I had read her reports and was anxious to meet her," Mary Donovan Corso recalled, having been "so impressed by her great courage." Instead, she found Virginia "unnecessarily terse, as if she was not particularly impressed with being awarded the DSC." It seems that Virginia neither courted glory nor dealt with it graciously.

SOE's Maurice Buckmaster also strongly recommended

Virginia for the French military decoration, the Croix de Guerre. He referred to her heroism in the field as "a most powerful factor in the harassing of enemy troops." Despite her American accent, memorable face, and prosthetic leg, she had spent much of the war behind enemy lines without being caught. True, she did not submit easily to discipline and liked to make up her own mind, but she had rendered "inestimable services to the Allied cause and is a very great friend of France." On March 16, 1946, France awarded Virginia the Croix de Guerre with Palm, a high-ranking medal for heroism in combat.

But Virginia did not want any awards or medals, and told one of her Resistance colleagues, "I don't want people to talk about what I did. Everything I did was for love of France, my second country."

CHAPTER 22

HOME

When Virginia returned to the United States in September 1945, she was a stranger in her own country. So why did she go back? To rest. To forget. And she went for Paul, too, who wanted to leave behind a Europe ravaged by war. She left with the respect and admiration of her colleagues and superiors and with the love of a good man.

War had fulfilled her. Could peace promise the same? It took time to recover from the years of stress, endurance, and semi-starvation. "She looked dreadful, and so much older," recalled her niece, Lorna, who was sixteen at the time. "We saw that the war had taken a lot out of her."

Sadly, reuniting with her mother after eight years apart was not quite the reviving tonic required. Virginia had never been the society daughter Mrs. Hall had wanted. She had not married, had no children, looked washed out, and was evidently in love with this Paul Goillot fellow, a man of humble background and mere high school education whose ambition was to open a restaurant.

Mrs. Hall was cold to Paul from the first time they met. Virginia tried to reason with her, arguing that Paul was a good man who was kind, clever, and funny, that he made her happy. Paul tried to win Mrs. Hall over—but in vain. Plans to marry were postponed. For all Virginia's rebelliousness, she did not go against her mother's wishes, although she refused to give Paul up. The compromise was that she would live a lie by concealing her relationship with him.

And so, two weeks after her return to the US, it was her mother, and she alone, who accompanied Virginia to a private ceremony in Bill Donovan's Washington, D.C., office in which she was awarded her DSC medal. Virginia wore all white, with a white chiffon scarf across her hair.

Donovan greeted the women in his general's uniform, no doubt saddened by the fact that the low-key occasion was to be the last of its kind. The irrepressible general had cited Virginia's heroism to President Truman in a valiant battle to save his beloved OSS from closure, but not even her remarkable track record could persuade the president to continue with the agency.

Virginia had resigned from the OSS three days before, stating that her mission was complete. She wrote in her letter of resignation on September 24, 1945, that she spoke six languages and hoped to serve her country again. "I am deeply interested in the future of intelligence work and would like my application to be considered in the event that an intelligence agency is established."

Just weeks after the OSS was abolished by President Truman

in late 1945 came revelations that the Soviets had been spying on the US government and its atomic bomb program. The discovery was humiliating for Washington leaders and laid bare the country's failures in intelligence gathering. As a consequence, in January 1946, Truman created the Central Intelligence Group, which would become the Central Intelligence Agency (CIA). Virginia was one of the first women to join. The agency was seen as a key "offensive weapon in an expanding Cold War" against Russia.

Virginia was dispatched to Italy, where she found herself working in the same offices in Venice as in the 1930s. Her mission as a GS-13 contract intelligence officer was to gather political and economic intelligence on Soviet infiltration into Italy. There was plenty to observe, with food riots in the streets and popular Communist politicians calling for general strikes. While yearning for a more active role, she diligently wrote reports on events in Italy, France, Greece, and Yugoslavia.

Virginia's role was restricted to mere desk-bound analysis, never her real strength, and she informed her superiors that she found the work "unsatisfactory." In July 1948, she resigned. She made it clear that she "preferred paramilitary work to foreign intelligence collection." Another likely reason was that Paul was unwilling to join her permanently in Italy.

In France, the investigations into Alesch were finally drawing to a close. When he was summoned back to court on May 25, 1948, to stand trial, crowds flocked to see him. It is unlikely that Virginia was among them—although we cannot rule out that she might have attended wearing one of her disguises. She would have seen her nemesis, then forty-two, still mocking and defiant.

Just as his American interrogators had done, the French secret service rejected Alesch's offer of intelligence on Abwehr officers in return for clemency. In fact, most unusually, former Abwehr sergeant Hugo Bleicher testified against him. Those few Resistance fighters who had survived his betrayal also gave evidence, including Germaine Guérin and Jean Rousset.

As an active CIA officer, Virginia could not appear as a witness, but it didn't matter. The case against Alesch was damning. He continued to claim his innocence, but the jury returned a verdict of guilty and a sentence of death by firing squad. His execution took place on February 25, 1949.

WHEN VIRGINIA RETURNED to the United States in July 1948, she expected to slot back into another job at the CIA. However, young college graduates had taken charge at the agency, and exploits from World War II were no longer respected in the way they had been. These officers shared a narrow idea of an intelligence operative as someone in their own image: young, male, and white. Virginia applied for another position and was judged by a senior officer to be "the most qualified person . . . I have ever interviewed." Yet, although she was given a few short missions abroad, there was nothing substantial for her. She found herself on the outside once again.

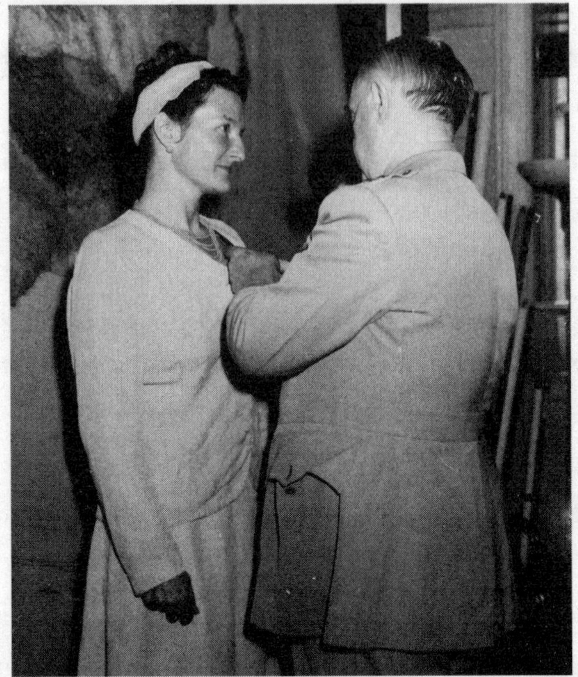

Top: Virginia receiving the Distinguished Service Cross for extraordinary heroism against the enemy from General William "Wild Bill" Donovan in Washington D.C., September 27, 1945.

Bottom: Virginia's mother, Mrs. Barbara Hall, accompanied Virginia when she received the DSC.

Early in 1950, around her forty-fourth birthday, Virginia moved to New York City to live with Paul in an apartment on 54th Street, near Manhattan's theater district. This was their first formal home together, and at least in the Big Apple they were away from her mother's disapproving looks. Virginia was much healthier now than she'd been when she first returned from Europe, and she invested in a new fashionable wardrobe. She and Paul had a large circle of friends, including a couple of ambassadors and a number of spies, and an invitation to one of their parties was considered a golden ticket.

Eventually the CIA came back to Virginia with an offer: a lowly desk job that was not even a permanent position. In March 1950, she started work as an administrative assistant at the National Committee for Free Europe, an organization that was a front for the CIA. From the third floor of the Empire State Building, she helped prepare broadcasts for Radio Free Europe, a propaganda station that supported resistance movements in Communist-controlled countries. It was repetitive work and not the paramilitary position she had requested, but after eighteen months of waiting, it was better than nothing.

CHAPTER 23

BEHIND THE DESK

In 1951, Virginia submitted yet another application for a job at the heart of the CIA. After months of vetting, including a lie detector test, she became one of the first women officers to be admitted to CIA headquarters. What was even more impressive was that she would be working for its less well-known covert operations section.

She and Paul packed up the Manhattan apartment and moved to Washington, D.C. They now saw more of her niece and nephew, whom they took on idyllic weekend trips sailing, fishing, and horseback riding at Solomons Island. Once, they rented a boat, and Paul caught eels and cooked them in butter on an open fire. He picked bunches of wildflowers for Virginia, and they all basked in the sun.

Virginia was always a self-controlled figure and never the cuddly sort. Lorna observed how her Aunt Dindy was unusually poised, sure of herself, and often surrounded by admirers. "She was a powerful person and ruled the roost, but Paul was good for her. He was a little crazy, a tease, always into mischief. They worked together brilliantly, and he lightened her life."

At last, Virginia found some satisfaction in her work, heading up ultra-secret anti-Communist operations in several European countries. She was responsible for overseeing recruitment and training of potential guerrilla units, as well as directing secret operations and organizing escape lines. Her exceptional experience was finally being put to good use.

Virginia's past was legendary among her colleagues, and she had become a "sacred presence" in a predominantly masculine world. But she was also a relic of what was already seen as a bygone age. One young male colleague described her as the "gung-ho lady left over from OSS days." Secretaries "in sweater sets and pearls listened raptly to Virginia Hall gas with muscular paramilitary officers who would stop by her desk to tell war stories," he recalled. "She was always jolly when she was around the old boys."

What is strange is that Virginia was not dispatched overseas to direct a major mission. It would have been in her character to jump at the chance. Instead, she informed her employers that she was not "interested at present" in a foreign posting—perhaps because she wanted to stay with Paul in the United States.

Over time, Virginia repeatedly asked for clarification of her duties, but she was told to be patient, and was gradually left to work in what she called a "total vacuum." Her suggestions for useful assignments were seized on as "fine ideas," and then handed to male officers to execute. Once, she was ordered to work on a task that, insultingly, entailed her reporting to a male officer two ranks her junior. For a war hero who had once been chosen over dozens of able-bodied men to conduct one of World War II's most dangerous secret missions, it was scarcely believable that within a decade she was being humiliated in this way.

A senior officer blocked any chance of Virginia being promoted with a scathing end-of-year review in 1956, despite admitting that he had never overseen any of her work. He denounced her results as "negligible" and claimed that she lacked "initiative, industry and creative thought." He posted the negative report immediately before going on leave, denying her the chance to discuss it. Not surprisingly, Virginia was furious and considered the report "almost incredible" and "unjustified." The way in which she had been belittled and ordered to report to a lower rank had been "improper," and questioning her capability in paramilitary work when she had excelled at it during the war was absurd.

The disagreement spoke volumes about how the ranks were closing against a woman whom less able or experienced men saw as a threat. Virginia's lack of recent field experience consistently counted against her, but even her critics noted that she was unusually adept at "picking out the flaws and pitfalls" of proposed operations—seemingly an all-too-rare talent at the agency at that time. Later, the CIA recognized that Virginia had more combat experience than most male officers, including five consecutive directors, and had been highly decorated for it too. Her shoddy treatment was cited as a textbook case of discrimination.

In January 1957, Virginia's morale improved when she moved to another CIA division, this time the Western Hemisphere desk. She was now an area operations officer, helping to run political and psychological warfare against Communism from Cuba down to Argentina.

Restored to some stability at work, she decided that the time had come to marry Paul. Her mother continued clinging to her prejudiced views, but finally Dindy cast her concern aside. On April 15, 1957, she and Paul gathered a few friends, drove out of town, and in a quiet, unfussy ceremony, got married. They did not inform her family until a couple of weeks later.

On Virginia's sixtieth birthday, the CIA's mandatory retirement age, she drove away from her parking space at CIA headquarters in Langley, Virginia, for the last time. Usually officers of her caliber and experience could expect to continue working as training consultants, but no such offer seems to have been made to Virginia. It was by any measure an unsatisfactory end to her career. Her many fans at the agency watched aghast as she packed up her desk and said goodbye. One of them angrily observed that "her experience and abilities were never properly utilized." Returning to such a humdrum world of rejection after her triumphs in the war had indeed been hard to bear.

Now that Virginia was retired, she and Paul had grand plans for their pretty home in Barnesville, Maryland. At last she could spend more time with their many friends. She took up gardening,

Virginia and Paul at their home.

building a greenhouse, growing vegetables, and planting thousands of daffodils. She and Paul kept geese and goats, and tried to make French-style cheese with the goats' milk. Cooking together was a favorite occupation—and after dinner Virginia would weave cloth on an old-fashioned handloom. It was a companionable existence.

Gradually Virginia's already-poor health deteriorated. She lost the strength and willpower to use her prosthetic leg, and Cuthbert was abandoned in a corner in favor of crutches. Soon she was spending most of her days in a chair watching the birds through the window and feeding her five French poodles from a silver ladle.

Her active brain devoured crossword puzzles, stacks of history and travel books, and especially spy stories. She refused to write her own tale, dismissing the idea with the unarguable fact that she had "seen too many corpses of colleagues who had talked."

When Paul was in his sixties, he suffered a severe stroke that changed his sunny personality into something darker and more gloomy. Both he and Virginia were now usually in pain and cantankerous, facing a daily struggle to cope. Virginia was in and out of the hospital for a complicated range of conditions. After sixteen years of retirement and thirty-eight years with Paul, Virginia Hall Goillot died, on July 8, 1982, at the Shady Grove Adventist Hospital in Rockville, Maryland, from unreported causes.

EPILOGUE

REMEMBERED

As so often happens, death triggered curiosity. The *Washington Post* carried an admiring obituary, describing Virginia as a "Baltimore schoolgirl who became a hero of the French Resistance." The *New York Times* called her "one of the most effective and reliable agents" of World War II. What they did not say—and could not have known—was just how a woman of no hope, no prospects, and apparently no importance had risen to such heights. How, in concealing her identity from others, she had discovered who she really was and what she really could do. How, in fighting for the liberty of another nation, she had found freedom for herself.

Four thousand miles away in France, the old boys from the Diane Irregulars wrote to each other to share the sad news. They had enjoyed nearly forty years of freedom since those months they spent with Virginia in 1944. The warrior they called La Madone had shown them hope, comradeship, courage, and how to be the best version of themselves—and they had never forgotten her.

The Diane Irregulars with their commander, Virginia, third from right, 1945.

Today, Virginia is recognized by the CIA as an undisputed heroine of World War II, whose career at the agency was held back by "frustrations with superiors who did not use her talents well." In June 1988, her name was added to the Military Intelligence Corps Hall of Fame, and in December 2016, the CIA named a building after her. New recruits are put through their paces in the Virginia Hall Expeditionary Center.

After persistent lobbying by her supporters in France and elsewhere, France and Britain celebrated Virginia's life in a ceremony at the French ambassador's residence in Washington, D.C., in December 2006. The French ambassador read a letter from France's president Jacques Chirac honoring her as an "American friend" of France. It was the first time the country publicly acknowledged Virginia as a "true hero of the French Resistance."

A painting by the artist Jeff Bass was unveiled at the event. It depicts Virginia in the summer of 1944, transmitting a radio message while Edmond Lebrat works the bicycle charger. To the end of their days, those who had known Virginia on the high plateau in France liked to pause now and then to think of the woman who never, ever gave up on their freedom.

ACKNOWLEDGMENTS

There were many highlights when researching this book, but spending memorable time with Virginia's niece Lorna Catling at her home in Baltimore tops the list. I am indebted to her for all the insights she gave me about her formidable aunt.

The hospitality extended by the kind and welcoming people of Le Chambon-sur-Lignon in France will also stay with me forever. Special thanks must go to Madame Denise Vallat, deputy mayor; historian Gérard Bollon; the staff of Le Lieu de Mémoire; Gabriel's widow; Madame Lebrat's daughter, Georgette; Michel Viallon; and Jean-Michel, who took time out to drive me around the plateau.

While in France, I was also lucky to meet Vincent Nouzille, an early champion of Virginia's. In Britain I have been fortunate to be guided by Steven Kippax. His knowledge of and passion for SOE knows no bounds, and he has helped me unlock old secrets and find my way through the world of intelligence. David Harrison has been a wise and patient counsel and font of knowledge about SOE. My thanks too to Paul McCue, who provided several useful pointers. I must also mention the superb resources and staff at the National Archives in Kew.

Pierre Tiller has been an invaluable consort through the maze of French archives. Régis Le Mer of the Centre d'Histoire de la Résistance et de la Déportation (CHRD) in Lyon made the Fayol papers available to me.

The staff at the Institutional Spy Museum in Washington, D.C., were wonderfully welcoming and kind (including the director, Peter Earnest).

I am grateful to Tony Duboudin, Alain's son, for talking frankly about his father, who, despite his flaws, was undoubtedly a brave man. Craig Gralley, a former CIA officer, has been a true support in my research. I am delighted to see his novel *Hall of Mirrors* do so well. The CIA's chief historian David Robarge cast his eye over the section concerning the agency and made helpful comments. Douglas Waller was also kind enough to read early drafts of the text pertaining to OSS, and I was honored to receive wise thoughts from the inimitable Lynne Olson. Alexander Noble also read through the text of the full version of this book, making further improvements. I am so grateful to them all. Stewart Emmens, Curator of Community Health at the Science Museum in London, was of help with his knowledge of historic prosthetics.

Tom White did a splendid job helping me with checking the early drafts. My son Laurie stepped in later, and showed me just what a great historian he already is. His younger brother Joe also contributed to the research—and egged me on to finish!

My thanks must also go to the following for helping in many different ways: Andrew Smith, Will Harris, Adam Fresco, Dr. Vicky Johnston, Paul Marston, Sarah Helm, Gina Lynn, Sarah Morgenthau, and Martyn Cox. Thanks too to Justin and Biz, Hilary Sunman and Peter Prynn, Paul Prynn, Gordon and Babeth, Tom and Anthony for their practical support in providing writing bolt-holes and emergency Wi-Fi—and everyone who has made me countless cups of coffee and mint tea.

My wonderful agent Gráinne Fox has believed in Virginia from the start, and the existence of this book has a lot to do with her energy and wisdom. My UK editor Sarah Savitt has been a great cheerleader for Virginia, and Andrea Schulz and Emily Wunderlich have kindly taken on that mantle from Joy de Menil in the United States. Thanks also to the remarkable Zoë Gullen in the UK and Jane Cavolina in the US for sterling work on the original book, and more recently Liz Hudson for her flair and dedication in adapting it for a younger audience, and Catherine Frank for her rigor and ambition. Thanks too to my publicists Grace Vincent and Rebecca Marsh for helping me get out there and tell the world about this exceptional woman.

Last but not least, I am grateful beyond words to my extended family for backing me on this book and putting up with me writing it. It means so much that my big sister Sue was thrilled about it before she left us. It means a great deal too that my husband, Jon, has helped and loved me more than I could ever deserve.

NOTES

Chapter 1: Dindy

"I must have liberty . . .": *Quid Nunc*.
"Second country": Translated testimony of Hubert Petiet, Nouzille, 14.
"Back door": From a conversation with her friend Elbridge Durbrow, in Rossiter, 190.
"It was her duty . . .": Catling interview.

Chapter 2: Living with Cuthbert

"Gentlewoman of great . . .": National Archives and Records Administration (NARA), RG 59, Virginia Hall, 123 File.

Chapter 3: A Chance Meeting

"It strikes me that . . .": SOE HS9-674/4, Virginia Hall's personal file, January 15, 1941.
"Considerable hostility . . .": SOE HS7-121, F Section History and Agents.
"Importance of looking . . .": Foot, 55.
"At the start . . .": Vomécourt, 86.

Chapter 4: Facing the Enemy

"I haven't yet seen . . .": *New York Post*, September 4, 1941.
"She seems to have . . .": Grose, 63.
"Preferred death to German . . .": NARA, RG 226, OSS Aid to the French Resistance.
"Undivided attention . . .": Virginia Hall's personal file, October 1941.
"Fires might mysteriously . . .": SOE HS8/1002, Report on British Circuits in France by Major Bourne-Paterson, 1946.

Chapter 5: Network of Danger

"Dark age . . .": Foot, 157.
"With little else . . .": F Section History and Agents.
"A small piece . . .": Virginia's personal file, May 5, 1942.
"Solidly established . . .": F Section History and Agents.
"Tart friends": Virginia Hall's personal file, December 4, 1941.

Chapter 6: Marie the Brave

"Grim undertaking . . .": Virginia Hall's personal file, October 8, 1941.
"If you could ever send . . .": Virginia Hall's personal file, March 3, 1942.
"You almost imagine . . .": Churchill, 180.
"Amazingly successful . . .": SOE HS7-122; Bourne-Paterson Report.
"Lay off": SOE HS9-631-2, Germaine Guérin's personal file (originally closed until 2031 but opened to allow research for this book).
"Knows everyone . . .": SOE HS9-314, Peter Churchill's personal file, vol. 1.
"Let's go": Churchill, 153.
"They're raiding the cafés . . .": Churchill, 153.

"Humming hive of hatred": Churchill, 153.
"When you get home . . .": Churchill, 153.

Chapter 7: Exposed

"We never despair . . .": Virginia Hall's personal file, January 5, 1942.
"Number one enemy": Cookridge, 602, referring to sworn documents signed by Germans on trial after the war.
"Still hoping for their victory . . .": Virginia Hall's personal file, March 3, 1942.
"She was paying . . .": Cowburn, 112.
"Very cordial . . .": SOE HS9-902/3, Marcel Leccia's personal file.
"Most special friend . . .": Virginia Hall's personal file, undated but probably October 1943.
"Stupefaction": Bourne-Paterson report.
"Her amazing personality . . .": NARA, RG 226, OSS Archives. Second draft report on Virginia Hall's honor from Lieutenant de Roussy de Sales to Lieutenant Colonel van der Stricht, December 13, 1944.

Chapter 8: A Pianist at Last

"A good executive . . .": Virginia Hall's personal file, March 3, 1942.
"We could use . . .": Virginia Hall's personal file, March 3, 1942.
"Man of nerve . . .": Foot, 190.
"Irritating acts . . .": Virginia Hall's personal file, January 18, 1943.
"I know my job . . .": SOE HS9-452-3, Georges Duboudin's personal file, May 17, 1942.
"What happens to soldiers . . .": SOE HS7-244, War Diary, F Section, July–September 1942, July 4, 1942.
"Outfit was completely . . .": War Diary, F Section, July–September 1942.
"Urging the importance . . .": War Diary, F Section, July–September 1942.
"Cease to exist . . .": War Diary, F Section, July–September 1942.

Chapter 9: Mission Impossible

"If they cannot come out . . .": Virginia Hall's personal file.
"I have a little present . . .": Langelaan, 161–162.
"A dilapidated, abandoned . . .": Ruby, 186.
"All Clan Cameron . . .": SOE HS8-171, Vic Circuit Signals, part 1.
"Lynchpin": Foot, ix.
"Very great number . . .": F Section memorandum, written on November 21, 1944.
"Many of our men . . .": Virginia Hall's personal file, October 19, 1942.

Chapter 10: Hunted

"An extremely important . . .": F Section History and Agents.
"Her kind heart . . .": War Diary, F Section, vol. 1, July–September 1942.
"Big bangs": War Diary, F Section, vol. 1, July–September 1942.
"A bluffer, vain . . .": Maurice Buckmaster in Duboudin's personal file.
"We are all vastly . . .": War Diary, F Section, vol. 1, July–September 1942.
"Can you check . . .": Virginia Hall's personal file, September 6, 1942.

Chapter 11: Infiltration

"I think my time . . .": Virginia Hall's personal file, September 30, 1942.
"I can't make . . .": Virginia Hall's personal file, September 30, 1942.
"Astounding personnages": Virginia Hall's personal file, September 30, 1942.
"Seized by panic . . .": Bourne-Paterson report.

Chapter 12: Escape to Spain

"Undocumented and destitute . . .": NARA, RG 59. US Department of State Central Files, Memorandum, March 2, 1943.
"Fiery love . . .": Simpson, 35.
"*Allô?* Who's there?": Thomas, 197–198.
"Best to you all . . .": Virginia Hall's personal file, November 25, 1942.
"Do everything possible . . .": Virginia Hall's personal file, December 4, 1942.
"For the life . . .": Simpson, 160.

Chapter 13: Burned

"Much of her usefulness . . .": Virginia Hall's personal file, July 8, 1943.
"You will see . . .": Virginia Hall's personal file, July 7, 1943.
"I have had the luck . . .": Virginia Hall's personal file, October 6, 1943.
"No reason . . .": Virginia Hall's personal file, January 28, 1944.

Chapter 14: Settling Scores

"He did not seem . . .": OSS Archives, Virginia Hall's activity report, September 30, 1944.
"I cooked for the . . .": Virginia Hall's activity report, September 30, 1944.
"Farmers and farm . . .": Virginia Hall's activity report, September 30, 1944.

Chapter 15: Betrayed

"Due to daily . . .": OSS Archives, OSS Signals, April 18, 1944.
"Very devoted . . .": OSS Archives, F Section, Rolls 6 and 7.
"Very hot": OSS Archives, OSS Aid to the French Resistance plus OSS, F Section.

Chapter 16: To Arms

"Period of activity . . .": SOE HS6-597, France Maquis, January–June 1944.
"Your daughter . . .": OSS Archives, June 2, 1944.
"Blessent mon coeur . . .": Vomécourt, 218.
"A wave of elation . . .": Buckmaster, 220.
"The same extraordinary woman . . .": Vomécourt, 224.
"Virginia was not . . .": Vomécourt, 224.
"Significant" forces: CAB 106-989, FFI Notes, National Archives, London.
"Leaving for parts . . .": OSS Archives, Aramis Activities in the Field Report, Saint-Heckler Circuit, F Section, Rolls 6 and 7.

Chapter 17: The Village on the High Plateau

"A trustworthy group . . .": OSS Archives, Virginia Hall's Activity Report, Saint-Heckler Circuit, F Section, Rolls 6 and 7.
"We didn't have . . .": Fayol, 137.
"Excellent and well-led . . .": OSS Archives, Saint-Heckler Circuit, F Section, Rolls 6 and 7.
"Remarkable calm": Fayol, 146.
"It's the English . . .": Translated from undated testimony from Eric Barbezat, Fonds Fayol.
"Nothing had been arranged . . .": OSS Archives, Marianne's testimony reported by Lieutenant George Schriver, in charge of inquiring as to whether Virginia should be decorated, December 6, 1944.
"Very British": OSS Archives, Marianne's testimony.
"Demanded no personal . . .": OSS Archives, Marianne's testimony.
"If I don't frighten . . .": OSS Archives, Marianne's testimony.

Chapter 18: The Madonna of the Mountains

"Very important figure . . .": Testimony from Georges Coutarel in Bollon, 54.
"She was very . . .": Translated letter Dédé Zurbach to Pierre Fayol, October 20, 1986, Fonds Fayol.
"This . . . operation . . .": Dédé in letter to Fayol, May 3, 1985, Fonds Fayol.

Chapter 19: Leading

"Diane breathed energy . . .": Nouzille, 290.
"[She] was not . . .": Dédé Zurbach, August 27, 1985, letter to Pierre Fayol, Fonds Fayol.
"Violently engaged . . .": Virginia Hall's personal file.
"This extremely courageous . . .": OSS Archives, Saint-Heckler report, F Section, Rolls 6 and 7.
"In view of . . .": Foreign Office SOE Adviser C. M. Woods of Room E 203 on September 26, 1985, in letter to Fayol, on 2nd lieutenant Henry D. Riley, Fonds Fayol.
"Pure slang": Dédé in letter to Fayol, October 20, 1986, Fonds Fayol.
"They shot a man . . .": Vomécourt, 19.

Chapter 20: The Boat on the Lake

"I held Diane . . .": Dédé to Fayol, January 24, 1991, Fonds Fayol.
"Tolerance, friendship . . .": Dédé to Fayol, May 3, 1985, Fonds Fayol.
"Stingy": Dédé to Fayol, October 20, 1986, Fonds Fayol.
"Virginia continues to be . . .": OSS Archives, Charlotte Norris to Barbara Hall, September 21, 1944.
"Diane, who crossed . . .": OSS Archives, Gerry (Caserta) to Chapin (Caserta), Sasac (Paris) for Brinckerhoff, March 25, 1945.
"Desire for independence": OSS Archives, Gerry to Baker (Annemasse) and Brinckerhoff (Paris), April 1, 1945; message from Gerry to Brinckerhoff, April 4, 1945.

Chapter 21: Survivors

"In my opinion . . .": OSS Archives, Virginia Hall's activity report.

"Inasmuch as an award . . .": OSS Archives, Telegram, May 10, 1945.
"Miss Virginia Hall . . .": OSS Archives, Telegram, June 13, 1945.
"I had read . . .": Rossiter, 125.
"A most powerful factor . . .": Virginia Hall's personal file, June 19, 1945.
"I don't want people . . .": Testimony of Hubert Petiet, in Nouzille, 14.

Chapter 22: Home

"She looked dreadful . . .": Catling interview.
"I am deeply interested . . .": OSS Archives, Resignation letter from Virginia Hall, September 24, 1945.
"Offensive weapon . . .": Leary, 5.
"Preferred paramilitary work . . .": Virginia Hall's official personnel folder, CIA.
"The most qualified . . .": Petticoat Panel Report 1953, CIA Reading Room.

Chapter 23: Behind the Desk

"She was a powerful . . .": Catling interview.
"Sacred presence": Recounted by Angus Thuermer in McIntosh, 26.
"Gung-ho lady . . .": Thuermer, in McIntosh, 126.
"In sweater sets . . .": Thuermer, in McIntosh, 126.
"She was always jolly . . .": Thuermer, in McIntosh, 126.
"Interested at present": Secret Personnel Qualification Questionnaire, January 1953, CIA.
"Negligible . . .": Virginia Hall's fitness report, December 28, 1956, CIA.
"Almost incredible . . .": Lyman Kirkpatrick Diary, vol. 3, January 1956–December 1958, CIA; Virginia's official personnel folder, CIA; Memorandum for the record by [Name redacted], PP Staff, CIA; Hall memorandum for the record, CIA.
"Picking out . . .": Lyman Kirkpatrick Diary, vol. 3, January 1956–December 1958, CIA; Virginia's official personnel folder, CIA; Memorandum for the record by [Name redacted], PP Staff, CIA; Hall memorandum for the record, CIA.
"Her experience and abilities . . .": Secret undated CIA report, newly released under Freedom of Information Act request, Virginia Hall's career in the Central Intelligence Group and CIA.

Epilogue

"Baltimore schoolgirl . . .": *Washington Post*, July 14, 1982.
"One of the most . . .": *New York Times*, July 15, 1982.
"Frustrations with superiors . . .": OSS Official Exhibition Catalogue.

SELECTED BIBLIOGRAPHY

Books

Bollon, Gérard. *Aperçus sur la Résistance armée en Yssingelais (1940/1945)*. Le Puy-en-Velay: Cahiers de la Haute-Loire, 1997.

Buckmaster, Maurice. *They Fought Alone: The Story of British Agents in France*. London: Odhams Press, 1958.

Churchill, Peter. *Duel of Wits*. London: Transworld Publications, 1955.

Cookridge, E. H., *Inside SOE: The First Full Story of Special Operations Executive in Western Europe, 1940–45*. London: Arthur Baker, 1966.

Cowburn, Benjamin. *No Cloak, No Dagger: Allied Spycraft in Occupied France*. London: Brown, Watson, 1960.

Fayol, Pierre. *Le Chambon-sur-Lignon sous l'occupation (1940–1944): Les résistances locales, l'aide interalliée, l'action de Virginia Hall (O.S.S.)*. Paris: L'Harmattan, 1990.

Foot, M. R. D. *SOE in France: An Account of the Work of the British Special Operations Executive in France, 1940–1944*. London: HMSO, 1968.

Grose, Peter. *A Good Place to Hide: How One Community Saved Thousands of Lives from the Nazis in WWII*. London: Nicholas Brealey, 2016.

Langelaan, George. *Knights of the Floating Silk*. London: Hutchinson, 1959.

Leary, William, ed. *The Central Intelligence Agency: History and Documents*. Tuscaloosa: University of Alabama Press, 2014.

McIntosh, Elizabeth P. *Sisterhood of Spies: The Women of the OSS*. Annapolis: Naval Institute Press, 1998.

Nouzille, Vincent. *L'espionne: Virginia Hall, une Américaine dans la guerre*. Paris: Arthème Fayard, 2007.

Rossiter, Margaret. *Women in the Resistance*. New York: Praeger, 1986.

Ruby, Marcel. *F Section, SOE: The Story of the Buckmaster Network*. London: Cooper, 1988.

Simpson, William. *I Burned My Fingers*. London: Putnam, 1955.

Thomas, Jack. *No Banners: The Story of Alfred and Henry Newton*. London: W. H. Allen, 1955.

Vomécourt, Philippe de. *Who Lived to See the Day: France in Arms, 1940–1945*. London: Hutchinson, 1961.

Periodicals

Quid Nunc magazine (school magazine), Roland Country Park School, Baltimore.

New York Post

Washington Post

New York Times

Interviews

Lorna Catling, interview with author at her Baltimore home, October 27, 2017.

Archives

CIA Archives

National Archives (UK)

OSS Archives, National Archives and Records Administration (US)

Centre d'Histoire de la Résistance et de la Déportation, Lyon, France

INDEX

Page numbers in *italics* indicate photos.